The Little Tool Box

for Anxiety, Anger, Depression, and Guilt
"Catch Your Teacher and Shut It Up"

By Francoise White

Disclaimer

This book is based on the author's personal experience, observation, and opinion. It is not intended to replace the services of qualified mental health professionals, or to diagnose, treat or cure any mental health condition or illness. If you are experiencing emotional problems which may pose a risk to yourself or others, please obtain care by a professional provider.

Copyright

Table of Contents

Introduction
Your Little Tool Box

When we buy a new computer, one of the first things we do to protect it is install anti-spyware, an anti-virus program, and a pop up blocker, all of which allow the computer to work properly while searching or visiting websites, feeling safe while focusing on the task at hand. Our brains are like wonderful computers that also need to be protected from negative thoughts that become like viruses and bacteria, invading the mind, body and eventually the spirit.

If you suffer from any one of these conditions (anxiety, anger, depression or guilt) you too need to install some kind of protective device that will allow you to live, work, play and concentrate on the task at hand with no distraction from these powerful feelings that can end up dictating your life.

If you are reading this, you probably have decided that you could use new tools to manage those negative emotions. Good thinking! After all, it takes tremendous energy and resources for the mind to grapple with scary, painful, debilitating and unwanted feelings. It drains the mind and when the mind is drained, so is the body. How much energy do you spend each day dealing with one or more of these dreadful emotions? How much energy are you wasting everyday investing all your body, mind and spirit into these negative thoughts that suck the life out of you? If your energy represented money, would you spend or invest most of it on something that guarantees you a negative return?

This book is about a simple, little, down-to-earth tool box which includes enough space for you to add in your own modified and specialized tools as we go along; tools handcrafted by yourself, for yourself. With this method you will learn how to set up pop-up blockers for the awful stories; if unconsciously we can make up terrible stories, consciously we can also change them into wonderful ideas. With the proper tools, we can learn to work with our emotions, rather than fighting against ourselves.

The Little Toolbox will guide you through awareness. You will re-invest your energy into getting some good, positive return, empowering you rather than taking power away from you.

Recognizing our emotions and thoughts when they pop up is a must

Being aware of what we think at all times is the key to blocking what we don't need. All it takes is a little practice, advice and being fully awake and conscious about what is happening right now in our mind. We need to monitor our mind and direct its traffic. We do not want our mind to wander on its own, it needs our guidance, and this is what we will accomplish with *The Little Toolbox*.

1
Teachers
Why Call Them Teachers?

We tend to think of teachers as individuals having earned that designation by obtaining a diploma or certification. Why then, do I designate emotions, entities or individuals as teachers when they so obviously lack a diploma or certificate? The answer is really quite simple. The teachers I have known in my life have taken many different forms but they have all had one major quality in common.

My teachers have unconsciously shown me that through any given situation, I have the opportunity to learn something, something about me. They do it unconsciously because they don't realize they are actually teaching. The fact that I am learning something from them earns them this title.

When I realize that each situation brings an opportunity to learn about myself, I can assign this title to the person or entity presenting the challenge. Doing this allows me to not get frustrated about the challenges that are presented to me, while clearly focusing on the lesson I need to learn. I know that I can always learn something through them. So instead of thinking they are all wrong, or wishing they would just leave me alone, I search for the lesson to be learned. I search for the information I need. I seek that which means something to me and will help me resolve my problems or see what my issues are.

With this definition of a teacher in mind, you are able to recognize, in many situations, the people who fulfill this role. My teachers are not ordinary, and they don't even know they are actually teaching me. They usually come in and out of my life, trying to push my buttons and thereby cause a reaction in me.

I feel confident that it will be similar with you. Some of them are always in your life, and more often than not they give you a lot of grief. They challenge you in ways that bring a lot of headaches while you learn to handle them. The obnoxious ones might be there simply to teach you how to stand up for yourself, or just say no. They might be there to teach you to remove yourself from unhealthy situations and disassociate from toxic people in general. They might teach you to take action or to take a break. They might bring out emotions in you that you need to address, like anger and guilt or doubt.

By looking at it from this point of view, our world is full of teachers, some good and some we would gladly do without. My own kids are my best teachers, and I have learned a lot about myself through them.

Emotions are teachers, too, and each one has a purpose in our lives. *Anxiety* will teach you to look at facts and evidence instead of illusions. *Anger* will make you feel your power inside and show you how you can use that force to be productive rather than destructive. Remember how being destructive destroys yourself in the process. *Depression* will put you in the right place to take care of your soul, nurture it and allow you to spend quality time with no distractions around. *Guilt* will teach you to look at your motives and intentions just to make sure that what you do is for the good of all.

So find your teachers. They are all around us and we all have them. You now have the tools needed in your toolbox to recognize them and discover what you are supposed to learn from them and most importantly what you are suppose to learn about you. So go discover your teachers and yourself. Life is a discovery process, be curious about it.

DISCOVER, DISCOVER, DISCOVER... YOU!

Recognizing Your Teachers

Let's talk about these nasty emotions that drain us, eventually make us sick, and often dominate too much of our lives for our liking. Some of us can even become addicted to these emotions. We can become a victim or fall into co-dependency without even realizing it. Emotions create a chemical chain reaction in our bodies. Good emotions create a good chemical reaction that feels good and is helpful to us while bad emotions result in chemical reactions that are unhealthy. If everyday we struggle with negative emotion our body gets accustomed to the unhealthy chemical reaction and will end up craving it, just like an addict craves that daily dose of drug.

We have had a long-time relationship with these emotions and that relationship has not been beneficial to us. It has adversely affected our bodies, minds, and therefore, our spirits. We are looking for a good relationship with these negatively perceived emotions; one that motivates us to grow, support this growth and most importantly, one we can understand and manage. We want a relationship that empowers us rather than drains us. We need to consciously establish a healthy relationship with these feelings and emotions, changing the biochemical make up of our brain.

So let's change that picture right now by letting me introduce to you some really great teachers – your teachers. Before we start, we must agree to treat these teachers with respect, honor, a sense of curiosity and gratitude. Yes, we must be thankful and appreciative of their teaching services, especially when we see them and feel them every day; so every day they give us the opportunity to change our relationship with them. It is just up to us.

Now, here come your teachers, and indeed you might recognize them by their commonly known names of Anxiety, Guilt, Anger, and Depression. Why do we call them "teachers?" Why should we see them as allies, instead of enemies? First of all, they are a part of us, an important part that will bring us many opportunities to learn about ourselves and discover healthy ways of dealing with challenges. In *The Little Toolbox* the reader will learn firsthand from the emotion's viewpoint. I present these emotions as great teachers, experts, whose stories have never been told. I will reveal their true nature, their purpose, their wisdom and their disguise. I share their secrets and defend their potential to teach us.

Anxiety will turn the reader into a private investigator, asking them to find facts or concrete evidence that something is really wrong. It will teach the reader to discern between fact and fiction.

Anger has the best disguise and is my favorite mentor.

Anger asks us to feel its strength, and not associate it with negativity. Anger tells us: "Recycle me; I am power, your power."

Depression asks us to pay attention to our forgotten soul. We will work with this teacher on pleasing our senses, our physical being. Our mind cannot resist and will soon follow.

Guilt asks us to look at our intentions and question them. Guilt also offers the reader a chance to investigate their actions and find solid evidence to see whether the guilt is justified or not.

These feelings are YOUR teachers, deserving of your respect and honor. Recognize them as a part of you that you want and need to change. This desire for change is why we are getting a toolbox and I am sure that after getting familiar with your tools, you will find you can use them for many other problems you might be facing as well. Yes, we are being proactive here, and we will be creative too. We will refine and modify our tools as needed. We will play games and have fun while catching any inappropriate ideas or thoughts, and reward ourselves for doing it and making it happen.

Something important to remember is that a variety of emotions live in every single one of us. We all have the same wide range of emotions living in our bodies, giving us ownership of those individual emotions. When an emotion vibrates in your body, it is YOURS, and that means you cannot blame others for you feeling it, even if they triggered that emotion. When you are feeling angry, anxious, guilty or depressed, it is

Your Anxiety, Your Guilt, Your Anger, Your Depression – in other words, Your Teacher. So, see that emotion as though it is your little tiny teacher. It is mysterious and you know it to be powerful too. Deep within, you know there is something more to it, something worth investigating. Let's say that it is a brilliant teacher with a great disguise, and it is yours, yours and nobody else's. But after learning how to use the tools in this book, you will have a personal security monitor that can recognize these emotions right away, waving a red flag when any of these teachers come up, reminding you to shut them up and not listen to their scary stories.

Let's start by examining your toolbox. The first thing you will notice, as part of this program, is that we are all starting with a brand new toolbox. You will discover that in the beginning, most of the tools will be used to help you understand and deal with your teacher. Are you ready? Ok then, let's open this brand new toolbox. Immediately upon opening it, you should see the few tools we have already gathered. They are the tools called Honor and Respect. Later you will use these tools to learn to honor and respect yourself, your whole self, which includes the body, mind, emotions, and spirit. As a result of honoring and respecting the other components of our being, your soul and spirit will automatically improve. In addition to the couple of tools in there, we can also add your willingness to do the work and that is really a very precious tool. We will also assign you the title of *Special Investigator* because we are going to investigate, so be curious and stay focused on the task at hand.

Can you guess what we are going to put in the toolbox next? Your teachers and yes, we will put all of them in there.

I want to outline some of the wonderful qualities these teachers possess. You need to be aware of their qualities and characteristics. This will allow you to know them better and learn to appreciate them.

Patience and dedication are the first two qualities in the description of your teachers. Yes, your teachers are very patient and most of all very dedicated. They have not let you down thus far and they will not go away until you learn the lesson. They are still here trying to teach you something. And how many years have they been with you? Yes, they are very patient and dedicated!

Another great quality about your teachers is that like no other teachers, they will come back to check on you even after you learned the lesson. They will check on you from time to time for the rest of your life and make sure you are doing ok. When they do come back to check on you, you had better have that toolbox handy!

Just imagine your teachers coming back to check on you after you have learned the lesson and there you are with your own toolbox, ready to show them you can use all the tools you have gathered and refined by yourself. Then you can spend a little time, but not much, with it and if everything is in order your teacher will be on its way.

Here is an example: You have learned your lesson and changed your draining relationship with these emotions, you feel more secure within yourself, well centered and grounded. Then you get a new job, a new relationship or a new place to live in and suddenly your mind is acting up again, firing many thoughts, questions, doubts and worries. This is your teacher testing you, and if you can stop your mind and all the negative thoughts from exploiting your being, your teacher will be on his way back to the toolbox. You will have succeeded.

Another quality of your teachers is the ability to change size, which they do quite a bit because they have fewer tools than you do. When your teacher changes size, it is usually only because they are desperate for your undivided attention. They don't know what else to do, so they make themselves big, bigger and biggest just trying to get your attention. They can get to be huge. They can get to be so big that they become scary, indeed very scary to us. When they are that huge, they end up spending most of their time in our faces saying, "Can you see me? I'm here to teach you something!" By this time, you almost cannot even see them for they have become too scary and too confusing. You feel lost in them because they have become too big and too draining. What has happened at this point is like a catch-22 because more teachers have come in to help the first one and that is what they do: ask each other for help.

So, if your teacher is anxiety, it may be that guilt, anger or depression will come in to help the first teacher. Remember they all are very dedicated to you and they won't go away until you learn the lesson.

Now you can get a grasp on how the process works and what your teacher is capable of doing. Good for you! The time has now come to put all the teachers in your toolbox. Are you ready? But wait! First we have to check on their sizes and see if they will fit in that box of yours. How do you feel about your teacher now? Just since you started reading, did it shrink?

By now you should see your emotions as your teachers.

You should be ready to listen and pay attention to them. Just feeling that way will reduce their size dramatically. They will get smaller and start saving precious energy for both of you. Yes, they do that too! Sometimes it helps to take a couple of big, deep breaths to bring in the oxygen which makes ourselves bigger and as a result, the teacher becomes automatically smaller.

All teachers are in manageable sizes now and we can put them to rest for a while in our toolbox. Believe me, they have earned a rest. As you are now aware, they really have been working hard and it is YOUR turn to take over this relationship with YOUR rules.

Your teachers will be very happy because not only have they been wondering when you would be getting your own toolbox, but they have also been questioning when you would finally be ready to take over that relationship. They have been especially curious about when you would grow, getting big enough for them to shrink and rest in your toolbox. They actually want you to get more tools; the more tools you have, the better it is for them because if you know how to use the tools then the teachers don't have to work as much.

So let's change all the turmoil and start our new relationship. You define that relationship in your own terms. Think about it – think about what you want from this new relationship. Don't make the mistake of thinking, "I don't want to be anxious anymore" or "I don't want to be angry." This is important because you need to empower yourself with this decision. Any "I don't want" statement is not empowering. Instead use statements like "I *want* to be free", "I *want* to trust", and "I *want* to be at peace and be happy."

Go ahead and take a peek into your toolbox. Notice that all the teachers are now in it, plus all their qualities – and remember this toolbox is all yours. The teachers' tools belong to you and are readily available for your use. The tools we see are respect, honor, patience, dedication, and willingness to do the work, plus the ability to change sizes – cool!! Let's be BIG! Being big keeps your teachers small while making them happy, and all of that is good for you.

2
Anxiety

The time has come for us to get closer to the teacher called Anxiety, but please, leave it in the toolbox while you do your homework!

Anxiety can eat you right up from the inside out and you know this remark to be true because of your "bad experiences" with this teacher. Apparently you didn't pay enough attention to your teacher because if you had, you would have noticed that this teacher carries a little sign with him. Have you noticed the sign? If not, gently move him over in the box and let him rest. Observe what he is laying on and note that it is a little feather bed looking so soft, warm and peaceful. Look again because that is not a feather bed at all but rather his little sign. Can you read it?

Here is a clue: if you do not have a concrete fact telling you, "Yes, there is something TRULY wrong here" then do not give yourself permission to be anxious. If you do not have any evidence, do not let your mind wander around trying to find something. You stop right there and say NO. You put your mind on pause. Read the sign out loud. What does it say?

"No fact = No anxiety"

Make your own sign now. In fact, make a lot of them and post them on your refrigerator, in your car, your bedroom and in your toolbox. I even give you permission to take your teacher's sign and replace it with your own. Now that you are working together and on your own terms, remember that your teacher's tools are for your use too.

What are you going to do the next time the teacher called Anxiety comes to you? As soon as you see it or feel it, decide to Not let it settle, do Not let it change size, do Not let it speak, and look for the sign. Can you see it? What does it say?

"No fact = No anxiety"

The biggest challenge here is to be able to immediately recognize your teacher and promptly take action. You may view it like a game called "catch your teacher." The only thing your teacher really wants is to be caught and put to rest in the toolbox. You will be struggling to catch it in the beginning, but you do have the advantage of knowing what anxiety is and how it feels. So, with all that practice at experiencing anxiety, you should be able to quickly recognize the teacher and catch him.

As soon as you start to feel Anxiety come in, you can identify it and pull out the sign. *No fact, no anxiety.* With practice, the game will soon become like playing hide and seek with the teacher. "Oh! I see you, teacher! Get the sign, get the sign!" An idea for your own sign could be: "Sorry teacher, I didn't get a fact, a fax, a phone call or any other evidence that something is wrong; so I have to let you go. Thanks anyway and bye-bye!" After you have told the teacher good-bye, and this is extremely important, tap yourself on the shoulder and say, "YES!" When I say YES in this context, I mean a big YES, a powerful YES, a YES that comes from deep within your belly. A YES that says, "I am winning", because you really are winning at that time. Celebrate that YES by making it big and happy! Did I mention big? Well, I meant bigger. And what happens when you get bigger? Yes, your teacher becomes smaller.

Notice your relationship evolving into something very different. Notice your teacher being happy to play games with you rather than trying to control you. Remember that compared to us, our teachers have a limited amount of tools. We have an unlimited amount of tools, so why not use our imaginations and make a game out of it? Play with it. I know you might not be able to grasp playing with it right away but you can learn to catch it right away.

With every catch you make, you must reward yourself according to the size of your teacher at the time of the catch. The bigger your catch is, the bigger is your reward. Rewarding your catch is a big part of this program as well as being a big part of your new and different relationship. The reward is very important because you need to validate your hard work, and no kidding this is hard work. It is probably the hardest work you will ever do in taking care of yourself, but you will emerge feeling like a winner. Being able to say, "I caught it, I caught it!" makes you a winner.

It may be that you don't feel comfortable with this plan of action and if that is the case, you can change it. If you don't like the idea of playing a game with something so serious, that you have struggled with for far too long, you can also view it as a test of your will. The rules for viewing it as a test are the same as for a game; you have to catch that teacher as soon as it shows itself to you and when you do, celebrate. "I passed the test, I passed the test!" You are an achiever of a goal!

As a reward, depending on the size of your teacher at the time of the catch, give yourself a grade ranging from an A+ to C-. In time, you will get better and better at passing the tests. Eventually you will know all the answers before you even take the test, thereby allowing you to pass with flying colors. Congratulations!

I would like to make a point here, a point that honors our differences. We all have different ways of dealing with private issues. I am not making light of any negative emotions because as I said earlier, I truly believe this is really the hardest kind of work to do. I am encouraging you to try to have fun with it because productive play while working is a more positive and motivating way of dealing with the work. A fun approach allows us to see this huge problem from a different angle and most importantly, deal with it while experiencing a different vibration. The vibration of fun keeps the other teachers away and permits us to accomplish a lot more in our endeavor to effectively deal with the problem.

Ideally, we want to deal with only one teacher at a time. In dealing with anxiety, we need to also explore the thoughts that come into our minds and appropriately deal with them too. Of course, the best action is to instantly catch the teacher and send it back to the toolbox where it belongs.

Regardless of whether you are able to catch the teacher or the thought, you are catching something. Most important, you are stopping the invasion of unhealthy thoughts and fabricated stories. Anxiety is here to teach us how to discern between fact and fiction, what is really happening and what is not. Anxiety asks us to stick to the facts.

You need to catch, examine, and change those thoughts into something better, much better. Again, you need to write your own story, your own script. If you are anxious about something with no evidence, no fact, no valid reason to be anxious, if you are worried that maybe you're going to be sick, lonely, betrayed, broke etc.; it is time to change the stories in those thoughts. Think nice, big and happy. If you are able to unconsciously make up a story that makes you feel anxious, then you also are able to consciously make up other stories with good outcomes. Work on changing those anxious or worrisome thoughts and then tap yourself on the shoulder.

I recommend catching the teacher as fast as you can without allowing it to say one word. Immediately think of your own story and stop the teachers from telling the story. You are the official storyteller now. Think about your stories with great bright colors. If you can, as soon as the anxious thought comes in, change the story. It is the same practice: the negative thought comes in, you say, "NO!" and replace that thought with a good outcome right away. If your thought is of a car accident, visualize people walking out of their car normally with smiles on their faces and no other vehicles around. If you think of an argument, visualize people having a great conversation, smiling, shaking hands and, don't forget, tapping each other on the shoulders. Keep these visions simple and clear. You don't need to make a big scenario and you don't need to have a lot of irrelevant stuff in your visions. Put your happy self in that picture. Put things that make you smile in that picture and use bright colors to imagine a big green meadow, a blue body of water, or a multi-colored field of flowers. Keep the panorama open and clear like a big blue sky with no clouds. It is your story, your script and finally YOUR LIFE.

I know from experience how truly harmful anxiety can be. Let me share with you a bit of my own life.

I am a Virgo and Virgos do tend to worry a lot. I used to worry about many things but mostly about my relationship with my ex-husband. We had arguments that would leave me drained, depressed and feeling empty of power for days. I do not know how many times a day I would think about seeing him and would associate that encounter with a dreadful argument. My thoughts were always negative and always connected with this painful feeling that I know to be anxiety. It was like a monster tearing me apart from the inside out. Even though I didn't see him every day, these thoughts would come to mind every day. I worried that he would show up and that of course we would fight.

As I said before I was anxious about a lot of other things but this one thing was the worst and maybe the best too. The worst because of the feeling associated with it, the best because it forced me to pay attention to my thoughts and realize how many times a day I was worrying. Even if occasionally I did have a real argument with my ex-husband, it didn't justify the state of anxiety I was experiencing every day. I honestly was getting tired and annoyed too. This energy, this feeling, was dominating my life and I had to put a stop to it. I couldn't go on waiting for and anticipating my next argument. It was getting ridiculous.

Finally, one day I said "No more, no more" and decided to close the door to all the negative thoughts coming in. I started to catch my thoughts as fast as they would come in. It was not a game for me – I was more in a survival mode, a mode to save my soul. I was very serious, dedicated and focused on that task. I wanted to survive, be free of this ridiculous state of mind and be free of the pain. I spent a lot of time stopping my negative thoughts, which was good because while I was concentrating on doing just that I was not anxious anymore.

Diminishing anxiety in my life was wonderfully good and refreshing for me. Every time a bad thought came in, I stopped it. "No, NO, No you are not coming in and ruining my life." Little by little I was able to get better and better at it to the point where now I am very good at it! It became a game: catch that teacher or thought. I was winning and I liked it. I was getting to be fast and accurate in playing the game. I started to add on to this process and not only would I catch the thought but I would also visualize a good outcome. After a while, it became a lot easier. I was slamming the door to the bad thoughts and opening another one for the good thoughts to come in! Stopping the thoughts and catching my teacher right away made room for positive feelings as well as dramatically shortening my anxiety episodes because I was concentrating on something else.

This process was very empowering to me. I could cope

and I was doing it! YES!!! No longer was I re-acting to somebody or something but rather I was being pro-active. I was engaging in behavior that resulted in doing the right and good thing for me.

I was empowering myself, finding my own tools, thereby honoring my soul and all of that felt really good. At the beginning we fight *against* the invader, and then we channel this power into fighting *for* something we really want rather than *against* something we don't want. By the end, we are not fighting at all. We are not *against* and we are not *for* anything. We just live for the good stories. We live for good experiences and we especially live for our dreams, so be sure to make them big!

Do not forget to also give yourself credit for facing and recognizing the invader, as this also represents an opportunity for empowerment. In the beginning the invader represents the bad things happening in your life, a person or a situation. Each situation you face gives you the opportunity to learn more about yourself. There is **No Exception** to this rule. It is up to you to pinpoint that opportunity to learn.

My best source of learning about myself has always been my children, who bring my emotions out all in the open for me to see; I like their way of teaching much better than the one my ex-husband used. He too brought my emotions all out, but with a very different vibe. If you look around at the people who are close to you, you will see that you can learn from the situations they make you face.

So, if in your close circle of friends or family, somebody always makes you feel anxious, angry, guilty or doubtful, look out and be curious – there is something there for you to learn. Learning about yourself is what it is all about, and you must keep your mind open to those opportunities of personal growth and learning. Anybody and everybody has the potential to help you learn. Even the biggest prankster you have ever met can teach you something, but only if you really want to learn,and in this case you might just learn to stay away from them!

Now let's look at the physical part of anxiety. It resides in your body so it also needs our attention. You have developed a physical way of reacting to anxiety. Try to identify that physical response of yours. What do you do physically when you are anxious? Does your body tense up, do you go around and around in circles, do you end up shaking, with headaches, stomach aches?

We need to address both sides of anxiety. The key is to examine how anxiety makes you feel, and pay attention to that particular sensation that literally vibrates your body. The emotional/mental response, as well as the physical response, needs our attention. We want it all to be different and new, so let's discuss what you can do to change this physical response. You should recognize in it a kind of pulsation similar to an adrenaline rush.

Yes, with anxiety, we experience some kind of a rush. For example, let's say you go the theatre to watch a horror movie. As the music gets louder, you know something scary is going to happen. Your heart begins to race, your breath gets faster, the palm of your hands get sweaty... you know the feeling. You are ready to scream and jump out of your chair at any second. This is very similar to what happens when you experience anxiety, but with anxiety it becomes a chronic feeling that eats away at your nerves without you being able to walk out of the theatre.

After discovering and identifying that state of agitation within myself, I realized that I was addicted to the rush that anxiety brings along. This was a great breakthrough for me. I was going to use this very important information, and I decided that since I liked that rush, I was going to get it on my own terms. Instead of getting it with unreasonable, scary stories told by my mind, I would make up my own, consciously. They would be big, exciting stories. It worked, and still does, to the point that now even when I feel an uncomfortable vibe that I am not sure of, if it feels bad I automatically associate it with something exciting that is going to happen.

I get my rush, but do not succumb to the fear of the uncomfortable sensation. When we get that sensation, fear is our automatic response. We may not know what it is, but we know we do not like that feeling. So use that feeling, there is Power in it, and this is what we are after. Put the fear aside, harvest the Power, and channel it into something you know to be beneficial – excitement and curiosity. You know the expression "having butterflies in your stomach?" Well, there is nothing scary about butterflies, they are beautiful, let them fly away. Use your imagination, become your own storyteller, the captain of your ship.

When you catch your teacher, you can clap your hands, sing, or whistle your favorite tune. Sometimes people give themselves a gentle tap on the forehead to break away and create a tender shock which helps direct your attention from the negative emotion to something that gives you pleasure. Any of these actions will push you away from reacting the same way you did before by creating a diversion. You can use distraction whenever you feel the need to break away from a negative emotion. Imagine you have a dog that is barking at nothing, and to stop it, you distract it by calling it, asking it to sit or play ball. The attention of the dog is now channeled into something more productive.

The physical act of diversion is also a way to physically celebrate your catch and more importantly, to really feel the good emotion that comes with it. Sincerely make the effort to put a lot of good, positive feeling into it. You are a winner! Jump up and down once... or twice, as YOU wish. In your thoughts, create a vision with a different physical response. See yourself celebrating your win with your arms pointing at the sky, and don't just visualize it, you should actually DO IT.

You want to *feel* the victory and all of its good vibrations, not just visualize it. In reality, it is very important to change the physical response. Simply saying to yourself, "I caught you, teacher, I caught you!" is a very easy but highly productive thing to do.

Remember to allow yourself to feel that joy of victory; revel in the power you feel within yourself at that time. Find a comparison for that joyous power. Imagine the feeling you must get when you catch the home run baseball at a national game. Imagine you just won at bingo or the lottery. Imagine a big win because when you catch the teacher, you have definitely won something big. That something big is your own power and it is priceless. You are not giving that power to anxiety any more. You are harvesting it and every time you catch your teacher and feel the victory, you become more powerful. When you become more powerful, your teacher gets smaller and both of you get happier. Yes!!!

As I mentioned earlier, emotions live within us and therefore we always have the ability to call an emotion back to feel it vibrating through our bodies. You can think about a past event and re-feel that emotion. Bring it back to life whenever you want because it is a great tool. Put that in your toolbox too!

If you have a hard time visualizing something joyously new, you can think about a pleasant experience of your past and bring it back to life. Bring that feeling of joy back. Fill your toolbox with all the many wonderful past experiences you can think of. Fill your toolbox with many good emotions and make them available whenever you need them.

Good feelings can come from all our senses so stay open to your senses. You can remember through smell, taste, sight, sound, and touch. Remember special melodies, songs and sounds as in your first concert. Remember seeing your kids when they were first born or the first time you saw the ocean. Remember any time you first saw a special person or place on earth. Remember the smell of the fresh baked bread, cookies or cinnamon rolls your mom used to bake. Remember touching and smelling your newborn baby or running your fingers through the warm sand. Remember touching your first puppy's soft coat with his furiously wagging tail, his tongue kissing your skin, the smell of puppy breath in your face... and so on. You get the picture!

We now have several tools in the box. We certainly have enough tools to be pro-active as well as enough to start effectively dealing with our problems. You might want to take a break and review the tools in your box. Carefully pick the tools that attract you the most. Choose the tools that make you feel bigger or excited or confident or happy.

We should also talk a little bit about being anxious but with evidence and facts justifying this state of anxiety; when something is actually really going badly, with no light in sight. And guess what! There is a lesson in this too! When we are faced with this situation, we need to recognize that part of this lesson is about finding out consciously that we are indeed not in control. And that is always a big deal for human beings. This is like other experiences, emotions and feelings we are talking about in this book.

But first, we need to feel the emotion and acknowledge it. We have to realize and accept the fact that we are not in control all the time. After we have tried everything we can, and nothing has moved or changed, we must let the universe do its thing, surrender to it and have faith that when the time is right it will change, because really everything eventually does change. So the best attitude to have in this situation after feeling the pain is always to stay positive, to visualize that it is going to turn out all right and really accept and recognize that sometimes we will face situations that we cannot change no matter what we do.

We have two choices here – we can succumb to the situation and feel badly, which is a normal and healthy response, but we cannot stay down. After a while we have to get back up and accept that we are not in control, that something really is wrong but we are not going to dwell on it forever. Instead we should concentrate on finding ways to resolve the situation in a way that is positive for everyone involved. The other choice is to feel bad, depressed, down and if we keep it that way we will eventually manifest the worst, therefore not helping in any way ourselves or the others involved.

Before we succumb to anything or anybody we have to look and see if there is anything we can do about it. What we can do is change ourselves and improve the way we face challenges. When we put our energy and emotions into something more positive, that may help to manifest a better result or it may not... but this is part of life. Let's take an example here: Somebody dear to you is very ill with a life threatening condition. What would be the best support you can give this person when you think about them? Would you rather imagine them sick and dying, or getting stronger and beating the disease? I prefer the latter.

When I thought of them, I would want to see them getting stronger and being comfortable. I would encourage them to share my faith and love, and let them know that no matter what, I am with them and they can use my good energy for themselves. So this way you are actually helping them and yourself too. You are manifesting and sending good energy to the loved one. This is healing in itself and you too can be a great healer, as we all have the capacity to be.

When we have reasons to be anxious, the emotions we feel are justified, so let's feel them all and acknowledge them. Be honest with yourself – admit how hard it is, how unfair it is, how much it hurts, how helpless you feel. But then stop and look at what you can do about it, if anything. Then it is time for accepting reality – yes, here too we have to look at the facts, and we are going to apply the same method we do when we are anxious with no particular reasons. At some point we have to stop the little voice and check the facts: What can I do? How can I help? What can be changed?

If you can do something give your mind that mission and channel your energy into accomplishing that goal. If not, accept it and move on after you have processed all these feelings. Don't get stuck into this – allow yourself the time you need and then give your mind a mission, something else to experience. This requires setting a goal and guiding your body, mind and spirit toward that goal. You need to be fully aware and attentive because you cannot allow your mind to wander on its own. Pay attention to what you are thinking all the time, and make sure you catch every thought that triggers bad feelings. You can filter these thoughts and yes, you can change them too.

The most important steps with anxiety are: Catch your teacher; shut it up, breathe, take time to celebrate the victory and tell your own story.

Remember the little sign:

NO FACT = NO ANXIETY

Recap of Chapter Two:
What to do When Anxiety is Knocking on Your Door

#1: Catch your teacher, slam the door and shut him up.
#2: Search for evidence. If no evidence, go to step #3.
    If anxiety is valid, first process emotions and find a better solution, then move on to step three.
#3: Celebrate your catch, just like as if you won the lottery.
#4: Breathe.
#5: Tell your own story. Make it big; fill it with positive thoughts and more importantly positive vibrations and emotions.
#6: Reward yourself.

You are encouraged to create your own sequence. This is just an example, a guideline. Use your imagination.

A Note on Choosing Your Battles

We cannot deny the power behind anger and with it the feeling of fighting.

This brings up something else we need to look at, a simple concept pretty easy to understand: fighting "*for*" or fighting "*against*." As human beings we have a long history of fighting "*against*," and we are very good at it. For centuries we have fought against other people's beliefs, religions, races, values, cultures, political views and what not. When we fight *against* others our focus and energy is directed at the other. When we fight *against*, we will automatically face some kind of resistance that is strong, aggressive and negative and directed back towards us.

What we should be aware of is that this negative energy is also affecting us. In this case two negatives do not make a positive. It makes a bigger mess for everybody to deal with. We have to look at the energy that is being created. So if one person is pissed off, his/her energy will be released into the world: if two people are pissed off at each other that energy will multiply by much more than two. They will feed on each other creating a much more potent and powerful negative energy.

This is not a pretty picture at all when you think that all of it is released into the world, our world, therefore affecting all of us. It is a sort of heavy pollution that we cannot see but certainly feel, consciously or not; it is here surrounding us all.

When we fight *against* others, the first mistake we make is to direct all our energy toward the enemy. We give our power away, we react to somebody's intense feeling when, as we have learned, we should stop and think about what is going on inside ourselves. We should take a step back and see whose crap we are dealing with and if any of it belong to us. If we don't, we get lost, and we are just driven to destroy something that does not belong to us – somebody else's caca.

On a physical level there are differences between fighting *against* rather than for.

When we fight *against* we need to protect ourselves, and so we become tight, rigid, and stiff and by doing so we limit ourselves from accessing our full power. To access the full power we need to be fully open. If we don't, we just have a limited amount at our disposal. The rest is hidden behind the door that we had to close for our protection.

The only time we should fight "against" is in self-defense

Now, fighting *"for"* has a very different vibration, for the simple reason that it is about something we really want, something we really believe in, rather than something we don't want anything to do with. Therefore when you fight *for*, you are all open, you want to feel it, you are not afraid, not rigid and you are ready to receive with body, mind and spirit all open.

Automatically, when we fight *for* we become bigger, all doors are open, energy is flowing and there is no blockage to limit us. Try to feel the two different feelings here and think about two different scenarios, one where you have to fight *against* and the other when you fight *for*. Notice the physical changes that occur when you feel one and then the other. We have to think about where we want to invest our energy, emotions and the rest of our being.

As we learned earlier, we want to direct our energy into something that will be healthy – that will inspire us, support us, nurture us and basically make us feel good. We also have to remember that the universe or human consciousness does not make the difference between good or bad energy, it receives both and will use both kinds. So when we are anti-war people and put all our energy into being anti-war, we have to realize that we are still feeding and putting power, energy into war.

The solution is to be *for* peace, to concentrate on peace and not give anything at all to the war. If you are anti-abortion, you are still feeding power to abortion. Instead, you can be *for* adoption, birth control, or abstinence. Again, deal with your emotions the same way you would with money. If you don't like war you are not going to invest your money into the war machine. If you want to be green you will likely invest your money into solar energy, wind, and water, and not petroleum products. You would make sure that not one penny of your money is spent on energy development that pollutes our environment.

This is the idea – walk your talk and invest both your money and energy into what you believe in rather than what you don't agree with. You will become more powerful if you invest all your being, meaning body, mind, spirit, emotions, thought processes, and money into what you feel is right.

If we look around we will find so many people wasting their energy on things they don't agree with – fighting *against* something is part of our daily routine.

We are great at finding and dissecting what we perceive as wrong, bad, negative and instead of just recognizing it and letting go of it we keep going after it, we dig deeper into it. We are fast to judge and condemn. We recruit others to be on our side to fight against, and we end up by manifesting battles everywhere.

Wherever we go we find things we do not agree with whether it is big or little, we notice and get outraged and are ready for battle. This creates internal and external war, first it happens in our mind, we are angry and we are going to stop these people! When the brain is engaged with this war it releases chemicals into our body that are unhealthy. We engage in this kind of war every day.

Our brain is hooked on finding ways to be at war, little ones and big ones. We don't like people at work and so we create an internal war in our brain; we cannot leave that person alone, we are going to watch and speculate on what they do, think, act like and we are not going to miss a bit. Every day we invest our body and mind into this particular person that we dislike. How about putting energy into the people you like and respect, you would get so much more benefit in return and would not manifest this negative energy around you and also inside of you.

The expression "I don't give a dime" illustrates what I am talking about, don't give a dime or an ounce of your precious energy to people, situation, idea you do not support and invest it in the thing you believe in. You will be a lot more healthy and successful. Be aware in your environment of anything that produces bad vibes and make sure you don't absorb any of it.

These energies are contagious just like the good vibes, except the bad ones are unhealthy. It is like a bad bacteria and can travel from one body to another, yes it is air borne and can travel and affect anybody who consciously, or more likely unconsciously, invites that energy by simply reacting to it. The best thing to do is to be aware of it and not be involved in it. You can look at the person and feel sorry for them because they are the one who have to live with that emotion and take it with them anywhere they go – you don't. You can be a witness but not a participant, you don't need to get involved and spread the disease around by reacting negatively to whatever it is.

Again, you need to be clear about what belongs to you and what does not; is it worth your time, your money, emotion, health or not? What kind of feeling will you get in return? If it is stress, anger, frustration, rage or migraine headache you obviously are not dealing with the situation in an effective way. But you can change that way, only you can. So, fighting "*for*" or "*against*"? I choose fighting *for* and will certainly fight *against* too, but only in self defense. Now, let's turn the page and get to know another one of our teachers.

3
Anger

I have to admit this teacher is my favorite! Yes, I have a real weakness for it. I think very highly of my favorite teacher and hopefully you will get to love it too. Why is anger a wonderful emotion? First of all, just to make it clear again, this is OUR feeling and we have to deal with it. Nobody else can. You deal with what is living inside of you – I deal with what is living inside of me. The same rule applies for everybody.

Anger is a wonderful emotion because when it hits you, if you are actually paying attention to it, you should feel the power instead of the anger. So from now on when you feel anger:

THINK POWER!

Let's see if right now you can recall a little incident in your past, a little "anger moment." You should be able to bring back that emotion and feel it again. Just... do it! We are not going to lose control here – stay with me. You are feeling YOUR power – it is like a surge of energy. Depending on how obsessed you are, you could probably generate

---

enough power to light up a whole city.

Do not visualize anger, because images are not what we want to associate it with; from now on we will forget the word anger. Anger is just the disguise for the great power underneath it, but you can use your power carefully and channel it into something good for you.

Remember the little sign Anxiety rests on in your toolbox? Well, Anger has its own resting spot, too. Let's open our box and gently move Anger aside for one moment, so we can get a look at its signs. One of the signs of our teacher Anger is:

RECYCLE ME!

We need to recycle this pure energy into something constructive, rather than destructive. This recycling requires us to own our emotions, and therefore own our power too. Remember the little kid who found something strange and didn't really know what to do with it? Well here we are again. We found anger and we're going to make it ours, because it is ours and nobody else's. My anger is mine, mine, mine! And from now on it is my POWER; mine, mine, mine, and nobody else's. Be possessive about your power. Don't give it away to anyone or anything. You keep it for yourself and use it well.

I want to share with you one of my personal "anger moments" followed by a realization. Several years ago I experienced an angry phase, which was scary too. It didn't have anything to do with my ex!

I had to renew my green card and register as a "good alien." I went to the immigration office to file my paperwork. The lady officer looked at my record and saw that eleven years earlier I had been stopped at the Canadian border, strip-searched and held for several hours, and finally released. Now, eleven years later, the officer told me they needed to investigate that incident a little bit more. She took my green card and put an expiration date of only one month from that day on it.

Terrified doesn't begin to describe how I felt. At that time, in the United States, a lot of people were being deported from every state in the union for similar reasons and some were being deported for no reason at all. I had been living here for fifteen years, had two kids, a house, and a strong business clientele. I was a responsible taxpayer! I was extremely worried about facing deportation.

At first all I could think about was that "stupid woman" who was my only contact at the immigration office. I blamed her and wished she could be sick and in a situation where no lawyers or doctors could help her. I was mean, enraged and surrounded by all my teachers (anxiety, depression, anger, guilt – you will meet the others soon). You'll see...

A few days later, my lawyer called me to let me know that the lady at the immigration office was not returning his calls. She was sick and no one else was familiar with my case. This is when I felt guilt come in!! I realized that my wish had come true and now I was having to deal with the unintended consequences... bummer! That is not really what I wanted. I just wanted to resolve my case and her being sick was not helping at all. Yes I was still angry and scared. I had to do something else with my anger and decided to put that energy to work for me rather than against me. So I decided to build a deck in front of my house, since I had always wanted one. It took me 3 days. I was working hard at pounding nails, sawing, carrying big pieces of lumber, and the whole nine yards. My anger was gone and what was left of it was my beautiful deck. Yes!!! After a couple of months, my immigration problem was resolved, I had learned a valuable lesson, and had something tangible to remind me every day that the energy of anger should be used to build, rather than destroy. Now, when I walk outside onto my front porch, I love it and I remember to recycle my anger into a constructive project. By the way, I also built a sauna with this teacher. I cleaned up my whole yard and cleared my garden of all the weeds. It is great!

After a while the anger dissipates but the power remains, and with this practice you too can harvest pure power for the benefit of all, including yourself. Later on, when you need the power you will be able to find it inside yourself without being angry, but at the beginning, when anger comes to you, you can learn from it and channel it into constructive things.

Anger is power!! This is the other sign that your teacher carries with him, and of course you could not see it because you were too angry to pay attention to these details. So remember to look for these two signs:

Recycle Me
&
Anger is Power

The rule with this teacher is basically the same as with the others, you want to catch him and certainly do not listen to him, not one bit. This one can tell some nasty stories...

stories that can hurt you and others too. So Anger is a bit trickier to deal with than some of the other teachers. You have to be quick to shut him up (allow no stories at all) and the tricky part is, you still want to feel that power.

The approach here is to consciously choose to be aware, but only physically. We choose to put the mind away and use the physical body to experience that power. It is very important here to keep the mind out of the picture – no thinking, no talking. Just listen to your body. You concentrate on feeling this wonderful energy, get in touch with it and think "My power – mine, mine, mine!!!" This big step allows you to understand your teacher's lesson and the gift it brings with it. It makes you realize how much inner power you already have and how much more you can generate, ideally when you need it, not when somebody triggers it.

So anger is a wonderful teacher because Anger teaches Power! We can now understand the good side of anger. What a relief!

It is very important to be patient with yourself during this process because it is going to take some practice before it comes easily to you. In the beginning you will need to focus on the wonderful energy by seeing through the disguise of anger and feeling your power. Once you make that connection and know this feeling to be power, Your Power, you can start getting your mind back into the picture and search for positive changes you can make with this pure energy.

Be careful with bringing your mind back in; indeed, you know the mind can be a terrible barrier and/or culprit! I often feel we would get better results by listening to our bodies rather than our minds. The mind can trick you, even lie to you, but your body will always speak the truth. Listen to your body. Your body knows YOUR truth, your body will always speak to you first and it cannot lie. When you make the right decision, your body feels good. When you make the wrong decision, your body feels bad. Listen to your body!

When we bring our minds back into the process, what we want is for our minds to make conscious choices. We need our minds to choose to use our power to make good things happen. We need to concentrate on what we want, rather than what we don't want. We also need to not concentrate on the person, place or thing that stirred us to feel anger in the first place. However, we do need to ask ourselves why we came to feel anger.

To find the answer to this question you need to find out how you got to the point of being so angry. Please don't bring in Joe or Jane Doe here; they really have nothing to do with YOUR anger. It is actually nobody's fault. Let's say it is just a misunderstanding between you and your mind, that naughty mind!

If we look carefully at the circumstances of how we came to feel anger, we will most likely find that it is because we are not using the right tool for the job. We probably can also see that we react automatically to this emotion. Maybe we throw things, hit things, or maybe we get lost in it (again automatically) because it is too big – we can't see beyond it or all we can see is red.

In this process, we want to change that automatic response. We are going to make a conscious decision to think and choose the appropriate response. If the mind were a motor vehicle, we would now be driving with a manual transmission. We would be consciously shifting gears and there would be no more automatic transmission to shift for us. We should stop the car, breathe deeply and only when we had taken enough deep breaths get back in first gear with all power available to us through all the other gears as we really need them.

So we stop and breathe while asking, "Why did I get so angry?" It was most likely because of your automatic transmission! With the manual transmission, we can shift gears and consciously slow down.

We can all find plenty of good reasons but none of them are going to fix our anger. Here, we don't care about the reason, we only care about the solution. We know that if you are feeling angry for whatever reason, it is just your true feeling. The fact remains; you are angry.

So is staying angry helping you in any way, even when it is justified because you have been used, abused, or betrayed? I doubt it; there nothing really helpful for you in hanging on to those feelings of hate and anger. Forgiving those who have hurt you is good for you, and you should try because it will release you of this burden, which is too heavy for anybody to carry for too long. Forgiving can be hard to do so while you practice, remember to catch your teacher and shut it up.

Reinvest your power into doing something that will have a positive outcome for yourself. Every time you think about what happened to you, or the person responsible for the abuse pops up in your mind, shut it up – stop it right there and make your own story. Realize you are in a different place now and you are not the same person anymore; let go of that anger because it will just keep on growing. The time is now to take good care of yourself, searching for better and different experiences. Open up to the new, you deserve it! Make it happen for yourself by letting go of people and feelings that you don't want anything to do with any more.

Yes you have a valid reason to be angry, but by staying angry you also become the victim of your own anger, so you are still a victim, not good for you. Do yourself a big favor, catch your teacher and shut it up and try to forgive the others, LET THEM GO!

So the real question is "who am I angry with?" And again, leave Joe and Jane Doe out of it. If they are angry too, it is their problem, not yours. The fact is when you are angry, you are fighting... and who are you fighting? YOURSELF! That is why it hurts so badly. Do you want to stop hurting so much? Then stop fighting yourself. If you fight yourself, you are never going to win... period.

This is an absolute rule with no exceptions. It is simply the fighting that makes these angry experiences so painful. STOP FIGHTING YOURSELF! Stop resisting and the pain will go away. You are fighting yourself because unconsciously you are not coming up with an appropriate answer or response to the situation you are facing. Plus, instead of seeing a teacher, you have just been seeing red... but not anymore because now you can read the signs.

You can now understand that by fighting yourself, you are wasting most or all of your power. Now you see that fighting and resisting yourself is not going to get you anywhere. Now that you have your toolbox, you can see and feel your power. Doesn't that feel better? So take all that energy in – don't blast it out and waste it on breaking things or wishing people ill. You take it all in and make a conscious decision to use it for your own good, which in turn should help you feel bigger and shrink your teacher! It is time to put that teacher in the toolbox for a well-deserved rest. We are now ready for the next step, so everybody take a deep breath...

The teacher is in the toolbox and we are going to leave it there. It is just you and me now. Let's see if you can already get in touch with your power through triggering it all by yourself. You can still use anger if you need it to help you learn through practice, but just for a little while longer. Soon, you have to try to bring it out in you without the anger part, just the power part. I know you can do it! Just be patient with practicing and learning this lesson. Practice, practice and more practice. Remember the lesson.

Anger says: Recycle me, I am your Power!

The teacher called anger brings another great gift as well. Remember, this teacher is a little tricky but if you can deal with it you will get so much in return. Anytime you find yourself face to face with any of the other teachers, you can count on anger to be on your side. That's right! If you are overwhelmed with anxiety, guilt, or depression and you finally get angry too, then use that anger, that power, to say no to the other teachers.

When you develop a good relationship with this teacher, the world is yours. You will learn to trust yourself. You will have the stimulation, the motivation, the dedication, the drive, and the peace you desire, because you will not need to fight this battle with yourself anymore.

You can fly with this teacher. Love your anger, love your power and therefore love yourself! Let your happy spirit soar! The power of anger can teach you all these wonderful things.

In honor of this powerful teacher whom I adore, honor, love and respect, I have a gift for you. My gift is a poem that I wrote in October 1999, describing a conversation between myself and my good friend Anger. At the beginning Anger speaks to me/you (verses 1-5) and at the end it is me/you (verses 6-9) talking to Anger.

Anger

Anger, anger I am.
Feel me,
I'm a part of you
I live inside of you
You've got to love me too.
Feel me now and I will teach you
How much I can do.
All you have to do;
Is see me as a part of you.

Anger, anger I am
You've got to live with me,
You cannot deny me
I live inside of you.
You've got to love me too.

Next time you feel me,
Please recognize me as a part of you.
And don't let it fool you, 'cause I can teach you
How to use me, for more power to you.

Anger, anger I am
I am not that ugly,
You have to look at me
For another kind of beauty.
I am a great teacher, my teaching is power.
Feel me now, I live inside of you
You've got to love me too.
And if you do, you will feel the power
I can give it to you.

Anger, anger I am
I am the great teacher,
the teacher of power.
Can you recognize me?
I am your great power,
You can do much with me.
You can channel me too,
Into something better
Into something for you.

Anger, anger I am
If you just can feel me,
Don't be afraid of me.
I have hidden beauty and a great big gift
That I will share with you.

If you can just see me,
I will make you feel, how much power
You really have in you.
And that is the truth.

Anger, anger
I can see you better,
I can feel your power.
I'm not afraid of you; I can use this power,
Some of it to love you and the rest for my soul.
I'm starting to like you,
I feel closer to you.
I do accept your gift,
With power I can do.

Anger, anger
I think I do love you
And it's been hard to do.
I really do owe you.
Cause this powerful tool,
Is gonna change me too.
Every time I feel you,
It will remind me too, to keep on loving you
And to use this power for loving me too.

Anger, anger
You have been with me for all this time.
I have learned to recognize you,
As a great power tool for my soul.
And I do not fear you.

I will use this tool,
In your honor, for you.
I will build with this tool
And renovate my soul.

Anger, anger
I do believe in you
And will never forget you.
Finally, I'm glad you are here, with me.
I can see your beauty
It is a part of me.
I cannot be afraid, not with you by my side.
I will feel forever
And enjoy my power inside.

Recap of Chapter Three:
What to do when Anger Pays You a Visit

#1: Catch your teacher, shut him up.

#2: Breathe.

#3: Feel just the energy, the power of it.

#4: Think power, YOURS.

#5: Give your mind a mission. Think about a way out of this situation.

You need to change something – you need to say no. You need to stand up for yourself and remove yourself from this kind of situation. Use your power to become assertive in making the necessary changes.

#6: Celebrate and reward yourself.

4
Depression

Let's begin our discussion of depression by looking at the dictionary definition provided by Dictionary.com Unabridged (v 1.1):

de·pres·sion Spelled Pronunciation[di-**presh**-*uh* n]
–noun
1. the act of depressing.
2. the state of being depressed.
3. a depressed or sunken place or part; an area lower than the surrounding surface.
4. sadness; gloom; dejection.
5. *Psychiatry.* A condition of general emotional dejection and withdrawal; sadness greater and more prolonged than that warranted by any objective reason. Compare CLINICAL DEPRESSION.
6. dullness or inactivity, as of trade.
7. *Economics.* A period during which business, employment, and stock-market values decline severely or remain at a very low level of activity.
8. the Depression. GREAT DEPRESSION.

9. *Pathology*. A low state of vital powers or functional activity.
10. *Astronomy*. The angular distance of a celestial body below the horizon; negative altitude.
11. *Surveying*. The angle between the line from an observer or instrument to an object below either of them and a horizontal line.
12. *Physical Geography*. An area completely or mostly surrounded by higher land, ordinarily having interior drainage and not conforming to the valley of a single stream.
13. *Meteorology*. An area of low atmospheric pressure.

Note the similarities between all the definitions in that every use of the word, the general sense of lowness appears. Sadness, gloomy feeling, hollow, sunken place or part, an area lower than the surrounding surface, low activity, low value, low state, negative altitude, below the line, surrounded by higher land, low pressure... every definition has some sense of lowness. The definition applicable to our purposes here is a lowness of the body, mind, and spirit.

Depression is a condition, while anxiety, anger, and guilt are emotions. Up to this point, we have been exploring those emotions and using them as a doorway to our souls. Let us now examine the emotions associated with depression, because this is where we will find our teacher, or more likely teacher(s). Some of the emotions associated with depression are: disappointment, sadness, shame, hopelessness, worthlessness and hopefully our good friend anger!

I say hopefully anger because in most cases when we are deeply depressed, we do not feel the powerful energy that anger represents. On the contrary, we feel more like we are paralyzed inside with no power at all. So if you are depressed and angry too, please use that anger. Remember that anger is an emotion of power. You probably can find other emotions or teachers associated with depression, like anxiety, guilt and doubt. We will call this teacher depression because of all the emotions associated with it. It's important for you to keep that in mind.

The first thing I think of when hearing the word emotion mentioned is that there are feelings in motion. When feelings are in motion it means they need movement and they need to be expressed. They need to be felt and not suppressed. (Don't let your feelings build a nest inside of you.) When we feel it, we know it. This is true for all emotions; you need to feel them to know them. Once you get acquainted with them, you will be less afraid of them.

When I say feeling them I mean it in a strong way. Really Feel these emotions. This is the key to understanding, just as it was with anger. Do not be afraid of your emotions – let them flow through your body. Feel them with your body, NOT YOUR MIND. (Terrible mind!) Think about this fear of dealing with emotions and ask yourself "what would be the worst thing I could find out?" What if you do find that you feel very anxious, angry, depressed and guilty? You already know that, don't you?

But now you have tools that make sense and are practical in helping you see your teachers more clearly. You can actually pay attention to your teachers (your emotions) and see through them by reading the signs. Don't forget to always read the signs!

Just like the other teachers, depression is asking for your attention . Depression can also get very big and will surely ask for help from all the other teachers. Remember that we are dealing with one teacher at a time and it is your job to decide which one you will choose. The one rule here is to choose the biggest one, because it is usually the one who calls for help. Consequently when you deal with the biggest teacher by paying attention to it, it will be happy and will send the other ones to rest in the toolbox, because really it wants all the attention. Does that make sense to you? Good!

Basically, none of your teachers are very positive storytellers and this one has an especially negative story. You are useless, incompetent, not worth the air you breathe... **Shut Depression Up!** You are not here to listen to this foolish story! Just as it was with anxiety, you will be able to change the story and write your own. With this teacher we are going to first use our bodily senses to get in touch with it and later, when the time is right, we will again use those same senses to free ourselves of it.

Allow yourself to feel depression physically. Do not let yourself think, just simply let your Body do what it is supposed to do. Let your body express itself fully, with no resistance from the mind. Let your body be free and your mind will follow. Since you are depressed, let yourself feel depressed; feel sad, feel disappointed, feel helpless, feel worthless, etc. Do you feel like crying? Then Cry! Let it all out; cry it all out. Cry it loud and cry it proud! Do you feel like screaming? That is anger! Use it well. Let your body express itself freely, all of it. We are going through the body first, and it is an indirect connection to the mind. Body first, then mind and spirit will follow.

By the way you should also do this exercise when you feel good. Don't just feel good but rather really feel it and make it bigger. Feel it in your body and then in your mind. This is where the mind comes in handy because it can help you make joy bigger. Yes, the mind is terrible but it can be wonderful too! You will see that by paying attention to your body you will not just feel good you will feel REALLY GOOD. When you bring the mind back in, it will acknowledge that good feeling. When both body and mind agree, it will feel VERY, very good; your spirit will be joyfully flying again.

The body is always the first one to talk to you and it will never lie to you. When you are feeling emotions, you are acknowledging the teacher and realizing it is a part of you. You do not deny its existence. You own it and it feels very happy because it belongs to you. At this time, you yourself might not be feeling quite as happy as your teacher, but keep it up – this is just the beginning. Bear in mind the first step is the biggest one and the hardest one too.

We have to focus our attention on being curious about our physical state. There are two stages here. During the first one you will stay inside your body and feel your teacher. During the second, the purpose is to notice how you act or re-act physically to this teacher. What do you see? Notice your posture, your energy level, your pain. Where do you carry it or feel it most in your body? To do this you might want to look from the outside in, as if you were watching somebody else.

Keep the mind out of any judgments (terrible mind); you are observing the physical state. You are neutral. You want to bring in your curiosity because you are discovering something new. It is actually new even if you have had depression for years. What is old is the way you looked at it or more accurately, the way you didn't look at it. Now we want it all, we want to know everything we can, we are pro-active and we are going to be curious about ourselves. We are going to find our treasure, our power and our souls. YES!

Depression is very common. We all get depressed some time in our lives and contrary to what the western medical model says, it is ok to be depressed. What is not ok is the way we address it. When we look at depression and think of it as a psychiatric disorder or the principal manifestation of a neurosis or psychosis, we are really ignoring the big and natural expression of our souls.

Depression is a time to nurture and care for the soul. This is why it is often associated with a lack of desire to socialize, the feeling of wanting to be left alone, and wanting to reduce our activities. When you need to nurture your soul, you need a quiet place for yourself, a place where you can listen to the silence and not be interacting with other peoples' energy. Activity and interactivity interferes with the purpose of spending quality time with ourselves. Sometimes we feel like sleeping for hours. If you feel this way then you should go sleep and cuddle with your soul because that is a good and healing thing to do. We need to acknowledge our soul and create a relationship with it; a good relationship where we care for, nurture and pay proper attention to our souls.

We are not robots and in a society where one week of

paid vacation per year is the standard, it's no wonder people get depressed. You are not alone. Yes, it would be great if the government and the medical field would acknowledge our souls in a meaningful way including their functions both locally and globally. Unfortunately we cannot depend on that, or on them, for this way of thinking but maybe we can teach them a thing or two about caring for souls. They probably need a reminder of the existence of their own souls.

People who have not forgotten their souls are easy to spot; they are the ones who will always try to empower themselves as well as anybody who comes into contact with them. This is a relationship we are looking for. We are looking for a team that empowers each other when working together. Most doctors do not think this way. On the contrary, they take power away from you by scaring you to death about conditions that are normal for you. It is by getting in touch with our emotions that we can feel and find out who we are. We cannot ignore our souls, we have to pay attention to their condition and we cannot do that with pills. So understand that depression is a time to nurture your soul and don't be afraid to do so.

Appreciate what comes with depression such as the inactivity, silence, and aloneness. These times are healthy in addition to being necessary for our growth and development. If you are not in this situation at home then you should seek a private place, or establish rules that will allow you to do so. Each of our teachers has two faces: one face of depression is quiet time, one-on-one nurturing, inactivity, demand for silence and a time for reflection on the soul. The other face is one of taking action. All the steps I outline are necessary before we can get into the work of taking action. We take action only after we accept responsibility for the condition of our own personal soul and have paid proper attention to it. Be curious.

When you feel depressed or lost, it is your soul talking – so listen, care for and nurture yourself which in turn cares for and nurtures your soul. It is our job to do so and it is also one of the tougher ones.

In this book we are developing a new relationship with our emotions and feelings by becoming aware of them, paying attention to them and understanding where they are coming from as well as what they are trying to teach us. Depression asks us to spend time alone with no distractions and in a state of silence. This allows each of us time to address our relationship with our individual souls. Spending quality time with the soul requires privacy. The soul needs one-on-one care, just like if you were caring for a little creature that is hungry and needs love. This one on one care does not need to be constant, we also need the nurturing and companionship of other soul to be healthy.

So what would you do if you were caring for this creature, this little baby soul? You would surely give it some love and support. You would ask questions like "How can I make you feel better?" "How can I help?" When people need care and support they will often tell you that just being there with them is healing and it makes them feel better. If you add to it the flowers, or chocolate, or music, or movie, etc... they will feel a lot better. They will also realize how lucky they are to have you around and they will be appreciative as well as thankful to you. This type of loving, empowering relationship is what your soul is looking for. There is a commonly heard cliché that basically says "Treat others the same way you would like to be treated." I have often thought the cliché would be much more helpful if the words of it were rearranged a bit because the real problem here is the way we treat ourselves. Why are you not treating yourself the same way you would treat your best friend? Treating yourself, your soul, in the same way you would treat someone special to you is a better way to approach your soul and start a relationship based on true love.

From now on when you are depressed, you need to nurture your soul and spend quality time with it. It needs special care and so do you. Your soul is your best friend. Don't try to ignore it because as your best friend and great teacher it is not going to go away. So deal with it!

If you feel uncomfortable with the concept of loving yourself, then forget about you, just care for that soul and think about all of us out here trying to make a better world, trying to empower all people and each other; we need you. We need you to accomplish this goal of caring for your soul and loving yourself; we need you on our side to make this earth a better place to live. We need you to plant more seeds in people's mind, seeds of respect (yourself first and then all others) as well as seeds of love and understanding; seeds of possibility and seeds of hope. You too can become a great gardener, harvesting and planting seeds all around. Depression can teach you that.

Embrace your depression, care for it and look at it from a very different angle. Look for the lesson, the time alone, the silence, the cuddling with your soul, and the love. Get yourself a flowerpot and plant seeds. Let them represent your soul; water them, feed them and grow yourself out of depression.

Next time you feel depressed realize you are not alone. Visualize all the people cuddling with their souls and caring for them like a little animal or baby that needs loving attention and keep your chocolate handy!

Remember just like your other teachers, depression will come back from time to time and check up on you but you will be ready to spend quality time with it. It will no longer be depression time. It will be snuggling time. It will be caring and loving time. It will be time from you, to you and more importantly, by you.

We have many reasons to be depressed and we must honor every one of them. They are all valid reasons and therefore we are not going to find out why you are depressed. Some of you probably know why you are depressed and some of you may not, but it doesn't matter, because this is not where the solution is going to be found. Often we need to address an event experienced in the past that resulted in depression.

If you are depressed because you have lost somebody, then you are grieving and this is also a time for nurturing your soul. But if you are depressed because of a bad experience that happened long ago, you have to let go and come back in the right here right now. We all know we cannot change the past; we have to accept it as gone. It is a fact. If you are depressed because you have a hard time letting go of negativity from the past, you need to practice letting go more often.

Here is a solution: Drink a lot of water every day and

hold it until you are quite sure your bladder is full, then run to the bathroom and experience how good it feels to let go. Every time you pee associate it with letting go of whatever you need to let go. Doesn't that feel good? Yes!!

Check and see with your physician if you have any condition that would be a contraindication to this exercise, such as urinary tract infection, kidney problems, etc.

I am very familiar with this process because I am one of these people who always run to the bathroom at the last minute and I am intimately aware of that great feeling of letting go. It is a good reminder, everyday! Let go, let go, let go several times a day, yeah! It does feel soooo goooood! And it brings you back in the right here right now. So pee and let go of the past.

We just talked about one of the signs that are so dear to our teacher:

Nurture that soul
Nurture that soul

Now let's read the other sign this wonderful teacher carries:

Depression takes action

This teacher called Depression, with the same old stories, can really put you to sleep and that is why you need to take action. Look closely at your teacher. I know you have not noticed its sign before; there was a big dark cloud around you. But look at it now; this teacher is not hiding its sign. On the contrary, it is frantically waving this sign in all directions because it is desperate for your attention. It wants you to take action; it wants you to take over. Any kind of action or exercise is very appropriate here.

Take Action

When you decide to feel your emotions, you are taking action. This is what you need to do. Again, make a conscious decision to do so. Make signs too, and be creative. Get yourself a puppet, a stuffed animal, troll, witch, rock, piece of wood or else a big flag with "take action" written on it... anything that will represent this teacher for you.

Another idea is to get something that represents action such as a fire truck, race car, toy soldiers, army truck, ambulance, a super man, wonder woman, action figure, etc. Engage in the action to go buy these things; you want something that will speak to you and remind you to TAKE ACTION. Perhaps you may choose something that reminds you of one of your heroes/heroines. Spend some time thinking about it. It can be anything that will motivate, stimulate, or even better, excite you.

Go get yourself a toolbox too, (one of those containers sold at a store that holds wrenches, hammers, screwdrivers and the like) because for this teacher we are going to collect a lot of tools. Yes, I am serious. Get a toolbox!

This is the kick-start. If it feels right and makes sense to you, you are already doing it. You can now put your mind back into it and think about what to get and put in that box. You are taking action and most importantly, you are taking care of you. You are empowering yourself with your actions. You are starting to understand what you can do and how you can do it. You can see your teacher more clearly now and are not afraid to shut it up. This is a huge accomplishment! Tap yourself on the shoulder. Reward yourself. You deserve it, big time! Note your teacher is getting smaller too.

I want you to also get ready for the next visit from your teacher. Be prepared, be aware, and be curious. Just like with the other teachers, always remember, it's very important that when you face your teacher, SHUT IT UP! Feel the teacher with your body for as long as you want and as long as your command for it to be silent remains in place.

You are now aware of your depressed state and you are feeling it with your body, but you have prepared yourself for this teacher's visit. You are ready to deal with it constructively. Remember what I said at the beginning: With this teacher we are going to use our body to first get in touch with it and later we will again use our body to get out of touch with it.

We are now ready for the part of this process, which involves getting out of touch with depression. You have been anticipating this visit and you have planned in advance for it. You seek out more tools and decide to get something good for your body because after all, your body deserves the best you can give it.

Things that make your body feel good have to do with the five senses, sight, sound, taste, smell, and touch. So maybe you will go out and buy some GOOD chocolate, good bread and cheese, a good wine... something delightful for your taste buds. You might also get some lavender oil or something else that smells good; food is included in this category as are perfume and flowers. You provide yourself with some good music, music you love and enjoy and it doesn't matter if it's meditative, jazz or rock n roll. Give yourself something nice to look at, such as candles or one of those funky lamps with colors and sparkles. Use your imagination and go shopping. You can find great stuff in second hand stores and at garage sales.

When you go shopping bring good emotions into the spree and think of it as you would if you were going to a treasure hunt because you are! Please your sense of touch with hot water such as in a bath, shower, Jacuzzi, steam, or sauna. How about massage? Have a professional, a friend or even just yourself massage you with your favorite cream, oil or lotion. The feel of your favorite shirt against your skin feels good too.

Create a collection of things to cater to each of your five senses. Have all these things handy in your toolbox and the next time your teacher shows up, you will be ready. You have an action plan here and you will indeed be ready for action.

For the next part of your action plan, you are going to set up a scenario: Your teacher shows up. You shut the teacher up and put a piece of that delicious chocolate in your mouth (it can also be a piece of jerky if this is what you really like.) Feel how GOOD it tastes, and let that feeling stay in your taste buds and in your body for as long as you can.

Concentrate and focus on that wonderful piece of chocolate. Mmmmm... yum this is soooo gooood. To keep that feeling going, you can have another piece. We are talking about one piece or two, don't go all day stuffing yourself eating chocolate, this will be counterproductive and unhealthy.

Another scenario you may choose to try is to take a bath and put lavender, ylang ylang, cedarwood, or rosewood essential oil in it. Smell the oil making sure the scent completely fills your nose. It smells soooo good. Stay with it, breathing the aroma deep into you. A good thing to know about the sense of smell is that it has the shortest nerve pathway to the brain. Smells go swiftly and directly to your brain. When you smell something pleasant, let your nose do its job. Don't think about it, just let the aroma speed to your brain. Spend some time with this sensation going on in your nose. Fully experience it; let it fill you with joy. If you feel ready, bring that wonderful mind in and say it out loud," This feels so good!"

By verbalizing the joy, you make it bigger and your teacher shrinks. Feel the hot bath water surround and caress your body. It's warm and safe so get all your tools out. Make bath time a uniquely special experience for your body's senses and for you. Bring your senses back to life in a big way and they will guide you to the right places. Bring in the glass of wine, the candle, the music, the funky lamp, whatever it takes for you to stay connected to your body and your senses. You breathe deep and you feel big. NO THINKING and SHUT THAT TEACHER UP. Catch it at every attempt it makes. You are spending quality time with your body.

Give your body a gift and get a massage. Get a facial to give your body a treat. Whatever you decide to use to treat your body specially has to be physical; there is still no mind in this picture. You eventually bring the mind back in when it is ready to say nice things such as "Yes, that does feel good, I want more, I love it, good job!"

There are other things that make us feel good physically, things we do every day but don't pay attention to, like... having a bowel movement, taking a pee, yes that's right and if you really want to feel good then hold it! Check with your doctor to make sure it is safe.

Here you get in touch with two emotions actually, one is the feeling good, the other one is letting go. This is really therapeutic and you don't need a doctor for that, it is free of charge! If you plan on holding it, again really feel how good it is to let go; the relief is wonderful, you are free, get in that state of mind and celebrate going to the bathroom, YES?

Let's go all the way and masturbate! Why not? It is physical and it feels good. A dear friend of mine calls it "safe sex with someone you love." Please keep the guilt teacher out of this one because masturbation is a valuable tool too. There is nothing wrong with it. It provides physical pleasure and that is what we are trying to accomplish so masturbation fits very well in this program!

A little note about wine, chocolate and sex: these are tools and we are not talking about a whole bottle of wine or pounds of chocolate, ok?! We are not turning to poor health by giving all our power to substances. We don't want you to end up in Sex Addicts Anonymous either. Moderation is the key. Plus, you have many tools available to you. Alternate them. Remember your health depends on consuming the right dose of medicine at the right time.

All through this book we have talked about focusing on, and paying attention to, teachers, emotions, body, re-actions and now taking action. Look at your life and you will find a lot of times when you are taking action. Pay attention to those times.

With depression we need to take action, so it's important

to notice your actions. You take action every day; empower yourself through these actions. Do you go to work every day? That is an action. Do you take a shower? That too is an action, and don't forget to allow your body and mind to feel good about that shower. Any action you take can be used to empower yourself. Don't just do it automatically, notice it and draw some power from it. If you have kids, you feed them, pick them up, wake them up: Action, action, action. Use your wonderful mind to acknowledge that you are taking action. Empower yourself, so you can take other actions to take care of this teacher called depression. Be aware of your strength; you find it in your every day life.

Another kind of action to take involves motivation, or the lack of it. If you have a problem getting motivated to action, which is very common in depression, set yourself up. Tell a friend you are committing to taking action about your depression and you want to go to the gym, take a walk, go bowling, play pool, go out. Tell them no matter what, you cannot refuse or make excuses not to go. Give them the permission to figuratively kick you out of your house. Tell them to remind you about catching your teacher. Give them a sign to carry so when they come in, they can wave it at you, reminding you to take action and get out the door. Explain the situation and make the same pledge to your friend as the one you made to your teacher and yourself. Get angry and feel your power; use it to motivate yourself. Just going outside and taking a walk can do you some good.

Taking Real Pleasure in Every Day Little Things

There are many little pleasures that we do not notice in

our everyday life. We need all these little treasures; they represent the doorway to a lot more satisfaction and happiness. Let's say you come home at the end of the day and you've had a terrible day. You put down your key, coat, mail and maybe take a pee!! Yeah, there is one of those little pleasures! Whether you have kids or not, set a rule to allow yourself, 5, 10, 15 minutes to sit down... sit down? Yes, there is another little gift here.

You know that good feeling when you sink into your comfy couch after a hard day at work. Ohhhhhhh, yeaaaah... I'm home! That is a little treasure moment. Don't let them go by without noticing and feeling them; embrace them. Spend time with them for they are your friends and you should pay attention to this kind of friend every day.

All these little treasure moments also play an important role in your well-being because not only do they bring you joy, but they also bring you into the right here, right now, which is the only place to be. It's the only place happening. Your future depends on the right here, right now. When your body experiences pleasure, whether it is big or small, it will always bring you back from the past or the future to be living at this present moment. Use these moments to come back into the here and now.

If you hate your job, see your break time as a little treasure! Use your break time not to hate your job but to love your break. Are you thirsty? Find a little treasure in the pleasure of a cool glass of water or something else you have been longing for. There are gifts everywhere. To find them, you have to shut the mind, stop, listen to your body and feel the good sensation.

If you pay attention, you will find in your everyday life there is a lot more good time than bad time. When you experience these little moments of pleasure, it is very important to acknowledge them mentally and register the feel good sensation in your brain as you feel it throughout your body.

When you watch your favorite TV show, cook your favorite food, read an entertaining book or magazine, or play that video game, stop before you begin; feel the excitement, the anticipation, the fun and let it register with the brain. Make it bigger and then when you play, you will enjoy it more. Keep it going big, bigger... biggest! **APPRECIATE** these treasure moments and **BE THANKFUL** for them with a big heart.

Everything we do here is bigger because if you look back at the dictionary and its definition of depression, we are reminded of a hollow or sunken place, or an area lower than the surrounding surface. This tells us we need to raise that sunken place, make it bigger, move to a higher position, promote growth and development, increase our force (power), restore to life, elevate, or lift up.

Putting cream on your face, hands, body, brushing your hair, brushing your teeth, washing your face with cold water in the morning are just a few of the things you can do. Acknowledge these little treasure moments by showing or expressing gratitude for each one of these little pleasurable actions. Elevate and lift up your spirit every time it feels good to your body.

All we are doing is changing the automatic response by paying attention to things we take for granted. We are remembering to be appreciative of simple, little things. Bigger is not always better, and in this case we want to start by taking time to smell the little flowers. They are all around us and will guide us to a bigger garden. All of us must plant those seeds, and if we do we will meet, sometime on this earth, a beautiful garden of people, all believing in other people, empowering and supporting each other. **YES WE CAN**, with only one seed at a time, because not one of us, including you, is alone.

The mind is a terrible thing to waste

As human beings we are getting invaded more and more by negative thoughts. It seems we cannot help it and I believe it does affect most of us. All that negativity eventually manifests into some sort of disease where literally we are not at ease with ourselves, our environment and even each other. This is bad news for the human race.

Like I said before, I see it as a very potent virus or bacteria – some airborne thing that little by little invades all of us. Once the bad thinking become a part of us, which basically is when we find ourselves struggling with certain emotion more often than not, we start to create more negative thoughts adding to what already exist. We are now surrounded by a big, negative cloud that we can call the human consciousness, and this big, dark cloud is polluting our body, mind and spirit. We are more and more receptive to this negative energy and unconsciously we absorb it without much questioning or realizing it.

So our sad human race is getting polluted by pesticides and chemicals that are mostly bad for our planet. Our food supply is genetically modified, (with more harmful chemicals and growth hormones) our medical system is giving us pills right and left, (most of them will "treat" one condition and give you a half dozen bad side effects) and the result? We are getting sicker and sicker. The high rate of cancer is almost seen as normal now, but it has actually risen by 300% since the 1950's.

So what can we do?

It all starts in our brain, our own little computer. Our brain is really a great computer. It is also a fact that we are using it at only 10% or so of its capability. WHOA!!

In our time most of us have a home computer and one of the first thing we do when we get one is to equipped it with all kind of anti-virus, anti-spyware software because if we don't, our computer gets invaded by all kinds of junk that eventually will freeze the machine and crash. Yes, we do that almost automatically, we are very aware of the risk.

So why not do the same with our own brain, yes we can set up our own spyware and make sure that we can filter our thoughts. This is really what I did with my anxiety, I became angry to the point that I could not allowed any more negative thoughts from coming in, it was a question of life and death, crash or live and live well.

My awareness became my anti-virus program, catching and filtering everything coming in. I used all the software available to me to concentrate on catching and filtering every single thought I had. It was like playing a ping-pong game at the beginning, it was like having pop-ups constantly, and blocking them constantly, but it worked. Day by day fewer and fewer pop-ups appeared. I could open the program I chose and focus on it without having to fight the invaders. Just like with a computer, if you don't have to worry about viruses, pops up and everything else, then you really can do much better work and concentrate on what counts. So imagine your life now with no anxiety or stress – which includes all the "bad" emotions we have talked about in this book.

Now we are left with challenges and the need to nurture ourselves and the ones we love, without passing on to them the viruses we had. Do not waste your mind, use it, it is a wonderful tool, give it a mission, the mission to stop all negative thought from entering your brain. YES YOU CAN!

An Inspiring Story

I have a cherished sister-friend that has been struggling for 50+ years with her family. Her relationship with her mother, sisters and brothers has brought her more stress and depression than anyone should have to endure. She was sexually abused at a young age and has worked to heal that wound for half a century. She moved as far as she could from her family in hopes of achieving more effective healing.

She settled in Montana, a place where Mother Earth is always available just minutes from town. She chose a place that allowed her to nurture herself in the company of Mother Nature and a place where she could always escape when in need of peace. She enjoyed the nurturing that came with no questions or blame.

Over the years she also found a community of strong, willing, and able women ready to support, listen to, care for and help each other on many different levels including mental, emotional, physical, spiritual and material. This feminine community represents her other family, the family that will be there for better and for worse, no matter what.

In sharp contrast, her blood family represents a gathering of teachers: anxiety, anger, depression, guilt and a lot of frustration. She had tried over the years to mend her blood family relationships, especially the one with her mom. Amy wanted her mom to acknowledge her father's abusive actions. She wanted her mom to admit she knew what her father had done to her. She wanted closure. She needed a mom who would be able to listen to her pain and love her as a daughter should be loved.

Unfortunately her mom refused to talk about this important issue and would not acknowledge any wrong doing by her husband in spite of the fact that the abuse sometimes took place when mom was physically present in the home. After years of therapy and a lot of good support from her friends in Montana, she survived and grew stronger but was still trying to understand where her mom was coming from as well as still longing and looking (even at age 50) for that special, unconditional maternal love she hadn't experienced.

Over the years nothing improved. Any emails or phone calls exchanged between family members would always result in an unpleasant and often dreadful conversation. Blaming others or ignoring the subject of abuse was the norm; rudely or abruptly hanging up the phone was the only closure to be expected.

With all these depressing relationships in her blood family, Amy was often left feeling totally lost as well as drained physically, emotionally, and mentally. However, her strong spirit would keep hanging on, refusing to give up; her strong spirit was her lifesaver.

One day she received a phone call from her mom. She was not there to take the call and her mom had left a message on the answering machine. After listening to the message she felt a kind of hopefulness about finally resolving the conflict concerning the abuse she had suffered. Her mom said she felt sorry for all the pain she had caused. Amy quickly called me and in amazement talked about this one chance to make things right. Amy wanted to think about what to say to her mom; she wanted to choose her sentences carefully.

We decided to take this opportunity to undeniably let her mom know that the phone message was the best present Amy had ever had in her 50+ years of life on this earth. Amy wanted her mom to know how very much the effort of that phone call meant to her. We decided that when Amy felt ready, she would call her mom and immediately thank her for this wonderful gift that had filled Amy's heart with love, gratitude and hope.

This was not an easy call to make by any means but after a couple of days, Amy felt ready and decided it was time to call her mom back. She had planned to not address the past, just talk about the present gift of that inspiring phone call in hopes of it leading to more serious discussions later about the negative family dynamics. Sadly, the phone conversation was cut short by mom abruptly hanging up, signaling to Amy that the answering machine message was not a sincere one.

Amy didn't even have time to thank her mom for the gift of the message before she hung up. All that wonderful hope Amy had felt went down the drain leaving nothing behind but depression in an ongoing teacher's conference of anxiety, guilt, frustration, sadness, anger... and still no mom in the picture. In addition, her brothers and sisters were still arguing and blaming each other every time something from the past came up. Mom was directing the plot from above making sure the blame didn't come her way. Amy was at the end of her rope with suicidal tendencies and no more resources to spare for her own survival.

One morning I was thinking about her; she had called me the day before to see what my plans were for the evening. She did not mention her deep state of depression but the next morning for some unknown reason, I knew I had to stop by and see her before going to the first farmer's market of the year.

When I walked into Amy's house, I immediately felt something was very wrong. I asked and Amy told me how bad her depression was. She had even gone to see a doctor for anti-depressant pills. She was feeling suicidal which was very scary because the last time she found herself in this situation was when she was 16 years old and she was now in her mid 50's.

We started to talk and I wanted to point out to her that the best thing to do was emotionally bury her family; she could count on her Montana family for love and support. We all want to have a solution in troubled times and some of her friends, including me, kept telling her our perceptions of the solution... the "what to do and what not to do" stuff. It always came out like "Amy, you can't bla bla bla" or "Amy you have to bla bla bla."

Amy reached the point where she could not deal with the "you have to do this" or "don't do that" stuff anymore. All her teachers surrounded her and there was no way she could do any more mental, emotional or even practical work for herself. So when I started to give my advice, she cut me right off in my suggesting what she could/should do or not do. She was letting me know right away about the way she felt.

I then realized I was using the wrong approach with her and yes, she had the right to be tired of people telling her how to resolve her family problems. I had just finished writing this chapter about depression and decided it was the perfect time for her to let go of the mental and center on the physical body.

I acknowledged her mental state and talked to her about what I wrote in this book. I first mentioned that even when the mind is not responsive due to being overwhelmed and in a deep state of depression, the body will always respond. So we needed to concentrate on and please the body.

I explained about the simple pleasures in life that we take for granted and pay too little attention to, like going pee and in this case holding it for as long as she could beforehand. We talked about washing our face in the morning and brushing our teeth and hair.

Amy was still in pajamas and was going through that morning routine with me. She began to focus on her body and all the things she was doing to it. She started to feel better about everything.

She imagined being inside of her body and rejoicing at feeling the cold water on her face or the massaging of her scalp when brushing her hair. She held on as long as she could before taking a pee and that too felt very good. She concentrated on making her body feel good. This took her mind out of the depressive state and allowed her to think about something else while still taking care of herself.

I mentioned to her that depression signifies the soul needing to be nurtured and gave her examples of how we could do that. I talked about visualizing all the people in the world cuddling with their souls and suggested we should get her something that would represent exactly that. Immediately she began to tell me about her teddy bear that was still stuffed in one of her boxes from the previous move. We went on to look for that treasure and after looking for several minutes she found it.

Things now looked totally different and much better; her body language had changed dramatically and she was tightly holding that teddy bear close to her heart. She was highly aware of holding her soul as we talked about this teddy bear representing her sad soul in need of nurturing and attention.

I told her to take her teddy bear everywhere we would go that day and to be protective of it meaning that if we went to my house and my kids asked to hold the bear, she had to think about whether she would let it go or not. I also told her that if she wanted to put it down, I would hold her soul myself and care for it while she was doing something else.

We went to a restaurant for breakfast and she had her bear on her lap the entire time. She would hold it to her heart and cuddle it using a lot of love and tenderness. She was feeling very good about it; she was reconnecting with her soul. Her nurturing instincts were kicking in, helping her to maternally care for herself and her soul.

During the day we also talked about the mother who was never there for her especially on an emotional level. We went back to when she was a little girl with no family support and no one to talk to about her huge problem. She told me that after the abuse she would often go outside where she could be alone, surrounded only by Mother Nature and there she would always feel safe. She learned to appreciate Mother Nature in a special and comforting way. She loved her way of feeling nurtured with not a word, just the sounds of birds and wind. She would listen to the sounds, feeling the warm sun on her skin and always feel a bit better.

Amy had very negative thoughts about her mother. She wished her dead. She knew she could not deal with any more phone calls or anything else to do with her mother. These feelings were intensely alive in her brain. After listening to how she would seek comfort after the episodes of abuse by finding refuge in nature, we realized she had found a new mother for her. Mother Nature always brought her a sense of safety, love and pleasure. She was a mother that was always there for her no matter what, a mother she could count on, a mother she knew would always make her feel better.

Back at home, we decided to do a ceremony to honor her soul and celebrate her new "mother." While I was setting up the sacred place to have the ceremony in, I told Amy to hold her bear and think about what it represented. While she was cuddling with her soul in the yard, I gathered some sage for the ceremony, to drive evil spirits away, as well as clear and purify the space. I gathered water for the taste buds, lavender oil for the nose, a nice bar of soap for the body, a clay figurine to represent the teacher, a great big Buddha in wood and the sounds of the outdoors plus the great Big Sky country which happened to be clear, warm and blue that day. We had a candle for the eyes to look at but also for the spirits around because they like candles as much as we do. I then called Amy in, and used the smoke of the sage to purify the sacred place as well as ourselves, while asking for three pledges from her: a pledge to honor her soul and the teddy bear for what it represented, a pledge to pay attention and nurture her soul when it showed signs of needing love and affection, and a pledge to always allow her soul to express emotions and freely feel them throughout her body.

We improvised all day and when it came time to celebrate her new mother I remembered that I had some asparagus to plant in my garden. What a great idea to honor the mother with a gift of organic asparagus in appreciation of all the healing she provided for Amy. We planted asparagus in Mother Earth as a gift with new ideas, opportunities, new intentions, gratitude and new understanding. The asparagus represented new growth and the process involved, including taking care of that new seed, (plant) such as the watering and fertilizing. This is the work involved before we can celebrate and see the fruits of our labor. This is all very hard work; do not kid yourself. The big challenge with depression is to address the body first because the mind is overwhelmed. By addressing the body we connect with ourselves without involving the mind and indirectly, by nurturing our body and making it feel good, we make our soul feel better too. So we basically use our body to connect with our precious soul. In the above story the teddy bear also represents our soul – we can use anything we want as long as we can consciously, directly or indirectly connect to that soul. Your participation is needed and crucial whether you deal with anxiety, anger, depression and guilt. Your awareness and acceptance is also key in this endeavor. Remember you are not alone.

As for Amy, to this day she still takes her teddy bear to bed with her; after all, it is her soul!

And she greets it every morning upon arising, acknowledging the living soul in her body. Yes, you go, girl!

Recap of Chapter Four:
What to do when Depression is Knocking at Your Door

#1: Catch the teacher and shut him up.

#2: Breath.

#3: Take action.

#4: Get your tools. You should be ready with this teacher and armed with good things for your senses.
Things like....chocolate!

#5: Focus on pleasing your senses, your body.

#6: Breath.

#7: Pay attention to how your body's senses are feeling.
Stay in contact with your physical self. Concentrate on how good it tastes, how good it feels, how nice it looks, how great is the smell, how wonderful is the music.

#8: When ready bring the mind back into the picture and verbalize what you are feeling, yes all the good things. Be proud of the changes you made and the action you are taking.

#9: Celebrate.

5
Guilt

Guilt is another emotion that needs our attention when it is out of control. Just like anxiety, this toxic feeling can take over our lives and our health. If you feel guilty about it every time you do something, then you must listen to what guilt has to teach you.

There are two kind of guilt: real guilt and funky guilt. Real guilt occurs when you really did or said something bad and is actually a healthy, normal reaction. This is pretty simple and everybody knows that when we do something wrong and nasty to somebody, we need to apologize and take responsibility for our actions.

While it may be hard to explain and actually say how sorry we truly are to the person in question, we understand that in some way we have violated a social or moral rule and feel the need to address it as well as correct it. Feeling guilty in this case is healthy and most importantly it pushes us to question our actions, while hopefully teaching us to not repeat our mistake.

We can frankly apologize while honestly saying we are sorry to John and Jane Doe. Now it is up to John and Jane to accept your gift and you might want to give them a little time to process their own emotions and feelings. From this point the ball is in their court and whether or not they accept your apology, you have done your job with integrity and honesty. For your part, you might want to review your actions, or think before you speak.

John and Jane now have the responsibility and opportunity to learn about their own values. Will they be able to let go, accept the apology and move on or will they be stuck, unwilling to let go? No matter what, it is now their responsibility and their lesson to deal with. In each situation presented to us, we all have the opportunity and responsibility to learn something about ourselves. It is our job to look at the way we act or react and stay in touch with how we feel, in order to deal with each particular challenge.

Funky guilt is associated with actually not being guilty of anything because whatever you did or didn't do, you didn't actually hurt anybody. You react automatically to this feeling by simply feeling guilty with no questions asked. This prevents you from giving yourself a chance to stop and question your actions. You also have created a physical response to this emotion.

We will address both of these automatic responses, the physical and the mental one. Our goal is to eliminate and replace all the automatic responses you have developed. By doing so you will be able to stop and objectively change your answer as well as attitude towards guilt.

The lesson with guilt is actually pretty simple: it keeps us in touch with our intentions. A bad intention says you are guilty, while a good intention says you are not guilty. The healthy question "What am I guilty of?" is the key here and that is why it is so important to allow yourself to stop and ask this question.

When you react automatically, you are bypassing this very important step and you don't see the stop sign. Guilt and anxiety ask you to stop and obey this rule, which allows you to consciously become aware as well as "in control" of this emotion. You will give yourself the chance to change the outcome. You will also give yourself the chance to not feel guilty when there are no valid reasons for it.

The Teacher guilt's sign is:

"Stop and Check Your Intention"

This sign is the teacher guilt's gift and helps us make sure we take action with good intentions for all. This gift keeps us on the right path.

The Right Path

We are on the right path when we consciously take care of ourselves first. When we live in the right here and the right now, we become aware of our emotions, thereby owning them. Being on the right path means we recognize our needs and allow ourselves to receive from ourselves first.

Many people who feel guilty are taking care of everybody else while paying little to no attention to their own needs. The fact is when we give from a full cup we give a healthy, organic and much more powerful gift, with great resources from the giver to the recipient. We can understand that this way is a lot more beneficial to both parties involved. It is up to you to make this conscious choice. If you want to give, then make it big as well as powerful, make sure your cup is full, and everybody will benefit. Giving/generosity is a wonderful action and should make you feel good, always. If you don't feel good and excited when you give then it becomes a toxic gift, resulting in a justifiably guilty feeling.

Feeling Guilty because...

We often find ourselves feeling guilty about not spending enough time with our children, family, spouse, friends, parents, dogs, cats... beings we love. This is a valid reasons to feel guilty. But first one must ask, "how much time are you really giving to yourself?" Do you have a full enough cup to invest your loving energy into others? Do you feel guilty because unconsciously you can't give anymore because your cup is empty?

Check your feelings and make sure you still feel good when giving because this will be an indication of whether or not you have enough in your cup to be giving at all.

If you don't feel good about the giving then it is time for you to pay more attention to your needs, to invest your energy wisely and keep the few last drops in your cup just for you. Investigate and find out if this is all you need, a little time just for you.

Once you have set time aside for yourself, you can decide how to make time for playing with the kids, taking the dog for a walk, visiting the parents, friends, etc. Sometimes all it takes is to just make a plan, and then sticking with the plan to make you feel better. For example, you could say to yourself "on Tuesday I will have a game night with the kids, once a month I will visit my parents, every week I will get a baby sitter and have a night out with my spouse."

So now you are planning and you are actually putting your mind into action. These actions should make you feel better because you are actually doing something about your guilt; you are not reacting automatically anymore. You are consciously managing your emotions and replacing the guilt by taking action. You are addressing guilt and giving yourself a new direction, thereby giving your mind a mission. When you do these things, be sure to feel good about yourself, and I mean really good!

To Mom and Dad

If you are a parent and feel guilty because you think you are not spending enough quality time with your children, you need to let them know by speaking your truth. You would be amazed to find out how much good will come just by being honest and telling them that you need to take care of yourself for a change, that you need time to decompress, or recharge your battery.

Gently remind them that you do take care of everything they see around them. They will understand because they see the things you do around the house. They also know you have a job and or other obligations. I have done that with my own kids. I was feeling anxious and guilty most of the time when anger came for a visit. Anger and frustration pushed me to question what was I doing wrong in my life and why was I feeling bad most of the time.

I realized I needed time for myself, good, personal, quality time to figure out what I needed to do differently. Even when I was angry (unconsciously at myself) I had to make sure my kids knew they hadn't done anything wrong; it was not their fault I was feeling bad. I always made a point of telling them really clearly that they didn't do anything wrong. It was just my mood and I needed to address it myself.

From the young ages of three and five years old until now, at fourteen and sixteen, my kids have understood that it was my problem, not theirs, to deal with. They would just go and do their own thing with no bad feeling, giving me the space I needed to take care of my emotions, and I did. So to this day I make the same statement, "I don't feel good, it is not your fault, you have not done anything wrong, and I need some space." You can use this statement for anybody and if they don't get it, it is their caca, not yours. Be clear.

Contagious Guilt

Guilt can be contagious, especially with children. They will feel the vibes and more often than not, they will feel guilty because they see you struggling and will think it is something they have done. Just like yourself, they might not think at all, and not look at their own actions to see if they have really done something bad. This pattern can be passed down to your kids. Make sure you let them know it is not their fault.

We can inherit guilt in that as parents we can pass it down to our children. This is all done on an unconscious level. We can inherit or give guilt, anxiety, and anger unconsciously. Did you inherit a pattern or belief system that is destructive to you and your loved one? Did you inherit guilt? Just by asking these questions you are now shifting from the unconscious to the conscious mind and this changes everything. It means you are not reacting automatically; you are more in charge of this situation. You are regaining your power and not giving it away to guilt, or anything else for that matter. Look into that guilt and find out if you inherited your guilt from family members or somebody else. Is someone trying and succeeding at encouraging you to feel guilty? Give your mind a mission: Where is that guilt coming from? Is it justified?

The good news is that asking these questions and wanting to find the answers is empowering in itself. So go for it, empower yourself, and know you are on the right track. Keep moving forward and don't blame others for your guilt even if you find out you inherited it. It is now yours to deal with. Recognize it as yours, accept it and most importantly, question it every time.

It is true that most people who experience guilt on a daily basis are good people with no intentions of hurting others. They unfortunately end up hurting themselves with a daily dose of unfounded guilt that is toxic to the body, mind and therefore, spirit too.

Anxiety and Guilt

Guilt usually comes with its best friend anxiety, and as we have learned from anxiety, we need to act fast to catch this teacher. Just like with anxiety we have to stop and investigate guilt. We are looking at finding out if we have committed a crime, and not just a crime, but a premeditated one. Did we intentionally hurt or destroy something or somebody? We are back to the conscious plane of looking at the intention behind the action. What was my intention? This simple question is the key to understanding the purpose of guilt, keeping you on the right path, and making sure that your actions are good. From here it should be easy to find your answer to "Am I guilty or not?" Stick to the facts and stay focused on your pure intention.

If your goal was pure, honest, and clear and you did what you did because it was necessary for your well-being or the well-being of somebody else that is in your care, then I pronounce you not guilty and you should do the same. This question and answer process is a challenge. We need honesty to be able to get to the root of why we acted this way and what the consequences of our action were.

Other People and Guilt

A great teaching really takes place here because the guilt we feel can also be associated with some pain we might have inflicted onto others. There are two sides here, and while we are going to take a peek at the other person's side, we mainly want to remain on our side and focus on our own "caca." In every situation it is each person's responsibility to be aware of what belongs to him or her and what does not.

We are still talking about the funky guilt where your intention was good and healthy for you or somebody in your care. This is where it should stop, but for us funky guilt people it is never enough. We worry about the other people involved and what they think about our action. If you take that road and try to find out what others feel, think or are going to do... good luck and make sure that you have a full cup of whatever, because you are going to invest your energy into something very draining and will most likely not find the answers to your questions. Why? – because it is not your job to do but theirs. You just have to stick to what is your responsibility in this matter.

There is another sign for guilt (I like caca better but you can use poop!):

"My Caca or Yours?"

The others also have a responsibility and opportunity here, just like you, to learn about themselves through this challenge. Once everybody takes a time out to process, an honest dialogue can follow hopefully bringing clarity to all involved.

In our daily life we can usually find someone trying, and often succeeding, in enabling you to feel guilty. This person will manipulate you into doing things you really don't want to do, and they will guilt trip you.

Be aware, and discern between what is your caca and theirs. Remember to check with your physical body before saying yes. If you feel bad and tense inside, you should say no. Your body is telling you clearly you don't want to do it. It does not feel good or right. Your body knows your truth; it will not lie to you and will always speak first, before the mind. Listen to your body for it has the right answer.

This also can be a very empowering experience and will surely be a challenge, but you will learn how to say no without guilt. You have a right and a responsibility to say NO when you don't feel good about doing something. You made the commitment to do or give only when it feels good. If you don't follow your commitment, what you end up doing or giving is toxic, and not good for anybody.

The manipulator might not even be aware of the guilt tripping they do and they might not have the right tools or knowledge to plainly ask for what they want or need. You do not have to judge them or think they are bad. See them as a teacher, someone here to remind you of the purpose of guilt: to check our motives, making sure they are for the good of all; to address and spot our caca and clean it up, to be clear and honest in our body, mind and spirit, with good intentions for all.

Strict Religious Upbringing and Guilt

I have learned something about guilt through many people I know who associate their guilt with a strict Catholic upbringing. This is very common, and I will put my two cents in on this matter.

One thing for sure is that it does not matter where your guilt is coming from, the only thing that matter is, "Is it justified or not?" Guilt in this case is perceived as a sin and if you grew up in this rigid environment, it is bad news. Well, the real homework for you here is to research the definition of sin, and most importantly the origin of it.

In Hebrew the word "sin" means to miss the target. When an archer would miss the bull's eye on the target, people would yell "Sin!" to indicate it was a mistake. The archer did not have to go to a priest to confess. He merely had to re-adjust and try again. This makes more sense. We are human beings and we make mistakes.

It is a refreshing fact of life to know that we will not always hit the bull's eye with our first try – sometimes we will miss. So the real question here is, "Did you miss the target on purpose?" The answer is probably no.

Jesus has already Paid for our Sins

I don't think Jesus was crucified to pay for me sitting here writing my book and feeling a bit guilty because I should clean my house instead. What do you think? I think Jesus paid for people who missed the target and did it on purpose. People who miss the target on purpose do so for the gain of power, in service to their ego and to the detriment of others.

Some people may take many lives in the process and never feel guilty about it. They are clearly committing a crime, not simply making a mistake. They act without good intentions. Accept your mistake as you would with a child and understand that there is not a set time in our lives when we simply stop making mistakes.

This would mean we are done learning, and that would be sad! If you are a true believer, then you know you have God's power in you, because he gave it to you. You don't need a middleman to access this power. If God is available to all who open their hearts to him, then you should feel it and this power should set you free. If you are not feeling that you can accomplish anything with him by your side, then you have given that power away to somebody or something. Yes, you can lose all that power to guilt, anxiety, anger, depression, substances and people too.

God's power is an energy accessible to all. It is faith that travels freely in the universe, for anybody to benefit by it. It is the power of Love flowing through your body. It is something you feel in your guts. It is a driving force, always available as an unlimited resource. Nobody can take that away from you except yourself, no matter what. If you believe in God or Mother Earth, the Universe, the Human Race, the Animal Kingdom, or just in Yourself, as long as you believe, you can achieve. When you believe in the good for all, that power is yours to use well.

The least you can do is acknowledge this force and do something positive and constructive with it; the worst you can do is nothing. So instead of investing the content of your cup into guilt, invest it into faith and yourself. I guarantee you will get a much better return on it.

My body is my temple on this earth; if my temple was soiled with negative energy and stress I wonder how receptive I could be to God's power, wisdom and love. If my temple is stressed out then I have closed my doors, and if the doors to my temple are shut, what kind of host am I? A host that shuts down their temple might not be very appealing to a Higher Power.

They may still be able to squeeze in, but having open doors would certainly be a lot more inviting. If you let go of guilt, anxiety and negative emotions you will open doors, and your temple will be bigger and brighter.

Let's Get Down and Dirty on Guilt

Guilt tricks you into wasting much precious time and life force that you could use for other beneficial purposes in your life with a greater return. Guilt is slowing you down, taking power away from you, confusing you, cheating you and, just like anxiety, eating you from the inside out. That's not a good picture!

Here is another form of guilt that might be more common than what we think. Some people experience guilt because in their eyes they are a lot more prosperous than others, and while we might think this is noble, that does not matter – it is still the "funky" kind of guilt. This is a great example of where we can see that guilt is stealing your happiness from you.

So instead of feeling thankful and having a daily dose of appreciation and gratitude for what we have, we feel guilty. In this case guilt is really unacceptable but still very real for the person experiencing it. It is their truth and they can't help it. Again it does not matter why you feel it, what matters is, "Is my guilt feeling justified and if not, what can I do about it?"

In this case, the solution is again simple. First, feel blessed for all you have, such as your kids, a home, a good job, food, water and all the basic necessities that some people do not have, and struggle every day to put their hands on.

So instead of feeling guilty you can replace that by feeling appreciation, luck, happiness and gratefulness. Make a donation by sending a check to a non-profit organization that takes care of the less fortunate – an easy yet meaningful thing to do. Volunteer your time to support a cause you believe in. Remind others of how they should feel grateful for what they have. Fortunate people need to be reminded of how lucky they are, and to never take their good fortune for granted. Spend time enjoying what you have and all the gifts that surround you. Don't let guilt take over your life and drive you into a state of despair. Focus on all you have to feel grateful about. Remember to give thanks to God, the

Universe, Mother Earth and Yourself too, just for recognizing that you are grateful. This will keep your cup full and you will be giving precious energy back to the universe for anybody's benefit. So, simply, I do thank you.

Changing the Automatic Response

I hope we are now getting better at understanding how important the step is of reading the stop sign, and actually stopping. It is crucial because this is where we bring in our conscious mind. This is how we come back to the right here, right now. This is where our true power lies, and at that time we want our power back.

We have to realize that in some way we have become junkies. Every day we need our dose of anxiety, guilt, anger or depression to survive and that is exactly what we do. We just barely survive on our daily doses, and we do all this unconsciously of course.

So the first steps are to recognize, as well as identify, the feeling of guilt and then stop. We breathe deep, catch the teacher, and stick it in the toolbox. Don't rush, for you will want to take pleasure in catching guilt and filling your cup at the same time. Be conscious about what you are doing and how it makes you feel.

When I catch one of my teachers I feel really good, I feel excited, happy, I celebrate and I feel big. I do not take my catch for granted; every time is a victory that I cherish. Every time you do that, you are in the right here, right now, and this is the only time and space that matters, as well as the only time your power is absolute.

Next, ask what your motives and intentions are, and what

do you want to get out of it? Take a couple of deep breaths before answering this question. Be honest and truthful. Your answer should be brief and clear.

When you know exactly what you need, you might also investigate some different way of accomplishing it that would feel better for you... a way where you might not feel guilty. Look for other opportunities and choices you might not have thought of. Now that you are aware and fully conscious, you will think more clearly. Give your mind a mission to find the best solution and focus on that rather than on guilt.

The physical reaction to guilt is easy to change because just by stopping and breathing you are changing each response. Change the mental response first, and then automatically your physical response changes by relaxing and calming down. When you catch your teacher this feeling of excitement or sense of accomplishment you get will also change your automatic physical reaction. As a result your body will produce different chemicals that are much better and healthier for your overall well-being.

Guilt and Anger

If you are lucky anger will gift you with a visit, for which you should say "Thank You!" Sometimes we reach our limit, leaving us feeling pushed and tired of other people relying on us and expecting us to always say yes. This is normal on their part, because more likely than not you have always said yes and they take it for granted.

If anger is visiting you, we can assume that your body has already been giving you many signs that saying yes in some cases did not feel good, and you have ignored these feelings. So now anger has to come to the rescue and is pushing you into action.

Finally, you have enough power to just say NO. Remember Anger is Power. In order to use it well you have to recycle it first into power, yielding an assertive "No" rather than an angry "No." Remember the anger is yours, and in this case you are probably angry for not standing up for yourself while letting yourself being taken advantage of. Do not direct your anger at the other person because you will get lost in it again.

When you say no, you are saying it for you. The other person is just a part of the teaching taking place right now, which gives you the opportunity to make it right for YOU. See the unconscious teacher in them, take the challenge and love your anger, your power.

Guilt is all about our intentions, so be clear about your intentions, make sure they are for the benefit of all, or at least for the benefit of most. Again, stick to the facts, listen to your feelings and be aware when you feel good about doing or giving – do not miss the opportunity to feel bigger and better. Use your mind to acknowledge these feelings, talk to yourself. Yes that feels gooooood, I like it, you go girl/man!

Also, of course, notice the opposite: when you feel bad and use your power to stand up and free yourself. You have a right and duty to say no.

Recap of Chapter Five:
What to do when Guilt Shows Up for a Visit

#1: Catch your teacher and shut him up.
#2: Search for evidence that can justify your guilt.
  What was your true intention?
  Good intention, go to step #3
#3: Celebrate your catch. Jump up and down, sing, whistle.
#4: Breathe.
#5: Be happy you are not guilty. Say yes!
#6: Reward yourself.

6
Our Body, Our Soul

What wonderful machines we all live in! Our bodies are our private temples, a gift received from the creator. It does not matter what size, age, color, texture it has, each body deserves full attention and reverence.

As a medical and therapeutic massage therapist, it has always been a privilege for me to be allowed to treat bodies. When I began this career something funny happened to me; I would just plainly be in love with each body after each treatment, I could not believe how good it made me feel.

After investigating this new feeling, I realized that I was just sensing the energy and the consciousness of the soul that resides in each one of us. The experience was and still is beyond words, making it very hard to describe. I was in a state of bliss. For me it was an honor. It was a state of peace and contentment where no questions existed and no needs of any kind were present.

I realized how important our bodies are – no longer just an amazing machine but a real temple housing a real soul as well. We each host a soul within our bodies. Unfortunately, we have become so cerebral that we take our bodies for granted. If we are not sick, in pain, too big, fat, or too skinny, we just don't pay proper attention to our wonderful bodies. We don't think about the water we drink, the air we breathe, the food we eat. We are fast at consuming any number of pills to get the fast fix. We don't even wonder about the side effects these substances have and how they can destroy or soil our temples. Everyone does it and the doctors on some level have become the caretakers of our temples.

Our brains are overworked while spending more time and consuming more energy on things that matter little. We are more and more stressed, being lost in a material world. Along with the stress comes anxiety, anger, fear, depression, guilt, and doubt, to name a few. This is not counting the long list of diseases associated with stress.

So what can we do about it? Well, if I could choose one function of the brain in our current time, it would be for that brain to just be able to read its body and the body's reaction to each situation we face. The brain can tell you when you are not overwhelmed by stress and what kind of energy your body is experiencing.

We are all familiar with body, mind and spirit. Notice the one listed first: the body, because the body is the first to assess the situation you are in. The body always lives in the present. It does not have any pre-set idea or values system. It will simply let you know what is happening right here and right now.

Your body is your personal, very sophisticated radar that can pick up on the atmosphere surrounding you, which includes the people and places encountered or frequented. Your body will never lie to you. It will always speak first, before the mind can interpret what is going on and eventually get lost in the thinking process. So listen to your body because your body knows your truth. If we can become more familiar with our emotions, accept them as ours, and deal with the issues that are pointed out to us, then we will free our mind of much unnecessary, draining work.

Basically it comes down to looking for and finding our own caca, addressing that and only that. You don't have to deal with anybody else's caca, it is not your job. You can point things out to people and you can guide your kids but you cannot, no matter what, take care of their caca. You can try but all you will get is pure crap that does not belong to you, and you can carry it forever and ever.

Liberate yourself from all the thinking by listening to the birds, the silence, meditating and emptying your mind once in a while. See your emotions as a great tool to find out who you are. Give your mind a mission to search and find out why you are so pissed off, anxious, depressed or feeling guilty thereby discovering if it is justified. Then use your mind again to find solutions.

Your mind needs a mission to perform correctly; you cannot let it wander on its own because it will get lost and take you down with it. You can play the same game of catch your teachers; you can catch your thoughts when you want to. If you find your mind wandering around and accumulating ideas with no good end to them, stop and give it a mission. Yes, you can be aware of your mind, be consciously aware of it, and you can direct and control its traffic.

Pills, Pills and More Pills

I just don't take pills, only aspirin once in a great while when I am in really acute pain. My body does not like pills and I think it is a blessing because it is forcing me to rely on alternative medicine. I would rather change my lifestyle, way of eating or thinking than take a pill to treat one condition with half a dozen side effects.

My kids are now 16 and 18, and the last time they saw a doctor was when they were new born, they have not missed a day of school because they were sick for years. Being an aromatherapist and using almost exclusively essential oils has been rewarding for our family, with no side effects! I like it this way, it is simple, easy and we pay attention to preventing ourselves from getting sick. We also eat organic food which I think in our time is a must. Keep your temple clean.

There are several things about the majority of pills that I really don't understand and don't support. There are the side effects – why would I take a pill for depression with a side effect that can make me feel suicidal? Why take a pain killer like acetaminophen, which is the leading cause of acute liver failure in this country? Why take a pill with so many destructive side effects that you have to take even more pills to address only the side effects.

Hum, I am wondering if money might have anything to do with it? Pharmaceutical drugs represent a multimillion dollar industry and have little to do with your health or mine; it is a business and its main purpose is to sell more pills.

Why make pills that are addictive – this is not for our health but rather somebody else's wallet, don't you think?

Yes, please think about it and research the drugs that you are taking, surf the web and make a choice based on how many goodies you are going to get out of that pill and what is the price tag? Consider giving away kidneys or liver, sex drive, or bone density, or having diarrhea, nausea, headaches, to name very few.

You could also become a junky with all these truly wonderful pain killers that cause more deaths than guns, cocaine, or heroin that are just as addictive too. Shouldn't we be healthier by now with all the pills we are taking, how come we keep on consuming more and more pills and we are not getting better? Where is the logic in all this?

Would it be worse to try natural, alternative medicine that will help us to clean out the toxins in our body, our temples, rather than just putting it in? Get on the web and search the pills and their side effects. Also check what are the alternative, natural remedies available. Again, be curious, this is a wonderful emotion to have and use.

Here are some web sites you can check for alternative medicine and also where you can find the truth about some pharmaceutical drugs and their real side effects, which have not been exposed to the general public. You will also get more information about the pharmaceutical industry:

http://www.henriettesherbal.com/
http://www.breggin.com/index.php?option=com_
    content&task=view&id=187
http://stopshrinks.org/
http://www.naturalnews.com/psychiatry.html

http://www.mindfully.org/Health/2003/Mad-In-America-
   Jun03.htm
http://www.shirleys-wellness-cafe.com/ama.htm
http://www.sntp.net/
http://www.wellnessresources.com
http://psychwatch.blogspot.com/
http://www.holisticonline.com

7
Making Our Own Choices

Throughout this process, we become more in touch with ourselves and rather than reacting to situations automatically, we first ask questions, and this is healthy because we also become aware of the different choices we have. By simply questioning our reaction and trying to find out how can we change our behavior or the way we look at the situation and the way we feel about it, we seek answers and the reward is to find some alternative to the issue we are facing.

In this chapter we are going to look at words and the impact they have on us, and replace them with other words that bring out different feelings in us.

Depression – Yuck

When I say the word depression, this word takes me down, it makes me sink and feel sick, and as a result I do feel depressed. Everybody understands the meaning of it and the feeling associated with it and nobody likes it. It is too dark, too heavy and will take you right into a state of depression. I have replaced it with "being in a state of nurturing your soul" because that describes to me the situation and also it points to the solution. I like it better; it gives me a different feeling, paying attention to our soul and comforting it. It is softer, warmer and puts me on the right track of gently taking care of myself and my soul.

The word depression feels like there is no light at the end of the tunnel, and makes me feel uncomfortable. Plainly I just don't like it and more importantly I am aware of the feeling I experience with this word. "Nurturing my soul" is so different; I can do it better. It is not so hard and might even be fun, it is open to my imagination and my mind as to how can I nurture myself. Chocolate, that's one of them yeah!!! Hot baths, facials, music or just going home and getting in bed with a book, many choices out there and I like it this way.

When you use the word "depression" you are stuck fighting against it, but "nurturing your soul" makes you fight for it. When I say "depression" it stops everything in my head. I get down and am stuck with this bad feeling, with this weight and sadness. I prefer the option with the chocolate and only one or two, I let them melt in my mouth for as long as I can.

Again here you have to evaluate your physical condition, and be realistic about any health problems you may have, such as Type II Diabetes, problems with overweight, or a history of bulimia or other eating disorders.

Finally, declare your bad day! Yes, a great way to own our emotions is to name them and accept them – so don't be afraid to declare: yes, today is my bad day! Tell everybody: "today is my bad day!" People can all relate to it, we all have this kind of day, nothing to hide about it. It is here today and it is mine, so bite it.

When I have one of those days, I declare it and I own it. I do not have a lot of expectation during that particular time and do not want to engage myself in a lot of things. So I do the things that need to be done, hope for the best and make sure I have a little treat available during that day to at least participate actively in getting myself something good. I also ask some of my friends what is going on with our planets. Yes, they do affect us whether we believe in it or not and most likely than not, one of them is going retrograde or doing something else to us. I like that part because this is one place where I can freely blame the planets; it's not me, it's not me!

When the planets are doing something like that you can be sure that you are not alone, most people feel the effect of it. It can go from communication breaking down, appointment canceled, nothing happening when you want them to be moving, things to redo, revise, reorganize and many more. I always feel a little better when I know it is because of the planets.

So when you feel bad and declare your bad day check with the planets and other people too, you will probably find out you are not alone in this situation. I think it does help a little to know we are not alone in that hole and when we are in it every little bit helps. Most importantly, participate in these days and add a little something, it does not have to be big, to make you feel a little better.

Stress – Yuck, Yuck

This is another word with many bad feelings associated with it. When I say stress it is like when I say depression. This word is heavy, too heavy – it weighs a ton and I can't carry this one at all. This is also a word that makes billions of dollars for pharmaceutical companies!

All systems in the human body suffer from it. It does invade your whole being; not cool at all. This word is very popular and is present in our everyday life, too bad. Again, notice how your body reacts when saying it with the true feeling that is associated with it. I plainly don't like it, my guts are tight, I feel surrounded by a big black cloud that even penetrates the inside of my temple or body. YUCK, YUCK, YUCK and no more of it.

I like to change this word and replace it with "challenge," yes I like that better.

A challenge is lighter, it even brings some light in me rather than taking it all out of me.

A challenge I can take – it brings out my competitive spirit, my curiosity, and I feel bigger too. I am ready to face the challenging situation without carrying that extra weight that the word "stress" comes with. Stress seems to come in a bigger package with bunches of caca all connected together, it is like a big mass of shit.

We don't really want to connect with it or look at it in detail. We are aware of its size and we don't know where to start, it seems to be everywhere. We cannot separate it from everything else, it is all one big mess. "Challenges" seem smaller to me, I can see them in an orderly way.

With each issue separate from the other, it is a lot easier

to focus and deal with one at a time. It is friendlier and more clear. Challenge gets me involved, but stress makes me feel like a victim. Challenges feels to me like a beginning, stress feels like the end.

Challenge opens doors that stress closes
Challenge is fighting for;
Stress is fighting against

The Little Toolbox

8
Essential Oils For Your Mind
the Wonderful World of Aromatherapy

Essential oils are effective and if used correctly, they are also magical, practical and easy to use. Here is a good definition for aromatherapy by Jan Kusmirek: "The use of pure essential oils to seek to influence, to change or modify, mind, body or spirit; physiology or mood." I have been certified in Aromatherapy since 1996 and have used essential oils every day, in my home, with my kids, dogs and myself of course.

I am a true believer in natural medicine and especially Aromatherapy, simply because it works. I also use it with my patients as a medical massage therapist every day. Before starting my treatment, I make a custom blend according to the needs of the patient and have the client smell it. It is always accompanied by an "ahh," of pleasure, and the body language is affected right away. You can see the shoulder dropping, the body relaxing, and the brain shortly follows.

I have been diabetic for 35 years now and living in Montana for 25 years. I have never been hospitalized for my diabetes or any other reason, except when giving birth to my children. My children have not seen a doctor since they were newborns and are doing just fine at 16 and 18. Aromatherapy works. I have had strep infections, staph infections, viral and bacterial infections, and the flu in winter and again, did not need to see a doctor for any of it.

The pleasant feelings we experience when smelling essential oils, flowers, food or beverages have a predominantly psychological effect. The shortest pathway to the brain is through the nose. The only place in the body where nerve endings are exposed is in the nose.

We all have experienced smelling something good. When this happens, we just stop and can't help noticing not just the smell but also the physical, mental and emotional response it creates right away. We feel better, lighter, uplifted. Our behavior changes pretty fast, a great smell will change your mental state in no time. You have to consciously or unconsciously pay attention to it, your mind and body cannot resist. The smell will take you back to the right here – right now, the only place to be. It can erase what you were thinking about or how you felt one minute ago, just like that.

Close your eyes, inhale the oil and you will be transported into a different world, more manageable, more pleasurable and of course less stressful. Aromatherapy works. It can be a great tool to help you achieve the changes you need to make to improve your life and your health, whether physical, mental, or spiritual.

When treating a patient using aromatherapy, my best tool will always be my client's nose. When your nose likes a certain smell these will be the oils that will work best for you. It is nice to have more than one oil, and so I have created a list of oils for you to try. These oils are safe and easy to use, just smell them. Put a drop on your pillow, on the collar of your shirt, under your nose, sprinkle few drops in your living room, bedroom, or any room and enjoy.

You can use oils in a bath too – just run your bath and add about 10 drops to the water, but do not use citrus oils in the bath. All citrus oils irritate the skin, so do not apply directly to the skin. They are all uplifting, though, if used as a room spray or added to a little hot water in a bowl.

Recommended Essential Oils

Oils for *anxiety*: Bergamot, (citrus) Grapefruit, (citrus) Jasmine, Lavender, Lemon grass, Sweet marjoram, Orange oil, (citrus) Neroli, (citrus) Patchouli, Rose, Sandalwood, Vanilla, Ylang ylang, and Basil.

Oils for *anger or aggression*: Chamomile, Bergamot, Lavender, Marjoram, Ylang ylang, and Cedarwood.

Oils for *depression*: Basil, Clary sage, Geranium, Grapefruit, Jasmine, Lavender, Mandarin, Melissa, Orange, Patchouli, Rose, Sandalwood, Tangerine, and Ylang ylang.

Oils for *guilt*: Basil, Cedarwood, Chamomille, Clary sage, Eucalyptus, Fennel, Fir, Geranium, Ginger, Grapefruit, Lavender, Lemongrass, Melissa, Patchouli, Peppermint, Rosemary, Ylang ylang.

Using Essential Oils

It is time to play again, now with your oils. We are all different and one scent or pill might work on one person but not another, but in aromatherapy you have your nose to guide you. The goal is easy and simple – if your nose likes it, bingo you have the right oil. You do not have to adhere strictly to the list above, you can investigate and try different oils. As long as you feel released from your stress then it is working.

I encourage you to go and smell samples of oils (organic oils) from a health food store. There, you can evaluate the effect on yourself. I also encourage you to make your own blend, but I would not recommend using more than five oils in the mixture.

For some of you, just one oil might be right. So go play with your nose and oils, and find new effective tools that can help you to make the transition from feeling bad to feeling better and finally, really good. Be curious with all your senses. Start with your nose and do not stop here.

There are many books about aromatherapy. I will list only one: *The Aromatherapy Book*, by Jeanne Rose. This is my bible and it is very easy for anybody to understand and use. But again, search the book stores and see for yourself, many books are available and might fit your needs better. Have fun with your senses, and therefore yourself.

9
Now, Imagine

Imagine you now can stop your teachers anytime they show up; any teacher, any negative thoughts you have. Imagine you spend only a brief moment with them and are able to send them back in your tool box right away. Imagine now a full nation of people aware of what they think; aware that they have the power and freedom to capture and change their negative thoughts without poisoning their temple. Imagine how successful we could become with no more unhealthy, dirty mental activity and with the ability to control and regulate our thinking process. Imagine we have invested our brain activity into finding solution to our problems, into happiness and hope.

Imagine we the people, only fighting for, with nobody left to fight against. I believe we can do it, in fact we have to do it, in order to become more successful as a person, a family, a town, a nation and a human race.

The only tool we have is our mind; it is our secret weapon, it is more powerful than we can imagine. This might be the only true thing we can really control. So imagine again and again; we are all doing it with you.

We can all unite with our common goal of simply living in peace, but that peace must start in our own mind. We do not need to cast a vote, we do not need a title to validate our expertise, we do not need to be physically connected to know we are the majority, and we do not need money to be part of this spiritual revolution.

All we need is a brain with good intentions; a brain that is well directed, aware of its thoughts and guided by somebody just like you, who wants to participate into making their life better, this world better for all living beings.

To become successful in all ways of life, we must eradicate all the nasty thought in our mind.

You are what you think, so think good and it will be good for you and the rest of us too – and from the bottom of my heart I thank you!

Bibliography

American Psychological Association (APA):
    depression. (n.d.). Dictionary.com Unabridged (v 1.1).
    Retrieved August 02, 2008, from Dictionary.com web-
    site: http://dictionary.reference.com/browse/depression

Chicago Manual Style (CMS):
    depression. Dictionary.com. Dictionary.com Unabridged
    (v 1.1). Random House, Inc. http://dictionary.reference.
    com/browse/depression (accessed: August 02, 2008).

Modern Language Association (MLA):
    "depression." Dictionary.com Unabridged (v 1.1). Ran-
    dom House, Inc. 02 Aug. 2008. http://dictionary.refer-
    ence.com/browse/depression

The Little Toolbox

Acknowledgements

I would like to thank the following people for their help and support:

Sieglinde Gaertner-Sharbono, for getting this project started and on its feet before you answered your own calling.

Jane Grochowski, for being here when I didn't have an editor and stepping in when I really needed help.

Darla Torrez, who brought this book to its completion with excitement, commitment and attention to detail. I am looking forward to doing *The Little Tool Box for Parenting* with you. This book is ours, Darla.

Without my wonderful editors this book would not have come to life.

Katherine Trigonis, for the beautiful artwork from a beautiful artist. A special thank you for persevering and finishing the illustration while living with cerebellum atrophy.

You are an inspiration for all, Katherine...

To Amy and her courage to share her story and her teddy bear with me!

To Jim Coefield, freelancer with Art & Image Creative Resources. Thanks for putting all the pieces together and always reassuring me about getting it done on time.

To Ira Byock, who has supported this project from the beginning. Thanks for always answering my email and question, having you on my side made a big difference to me.

To Jodi Leslie, for endorsing the book right away after reading it.

To all the other John and Jane Does who participated by sharing their knowledge, opinion, stories, emotions, feedback and expertise.

You are my family, I love you!

And to my kids, Tosh and Gabrielle; my best teachers and favorite ones too! I love you!! Thank you for picking me.

About the Author

Francoise White was born in 1960 in Die, France. At age 16 her dad committed suicide while on anti-depression medication. Two years later, her mother was diagnosed with Crohn's Disease, and Francoise stayed home to help her mother raise her seven-year-old twin brothers. Her mother passed away within three years, and at the age of 18, Francoise became the guardian of her brothers.

Francoise recalls being emotionally numb during most of this time. After being hit so hard, she did not want to feel anything. She became like a rock, hard enough to keep on doing what she had to do and rigid enough to not let in any emotions in. Taking care of her brothers, work and house was plenty enough to deal with. She put her head down and her emotions aside and went to work. Her rock crumbled many times, with feelings of anger, despair, unfairness and grief. She rebuilt it repeatedly, thinking that not feeling anything was better at that time.

After two years, her older sister took over the guardianship; Francoise packed everything and started traveling in the Caribbean, Central America and then to the U.S. Francoise realized later in her life that at 18 years of age, she was already the typical depressed 40 year old woman, with a job and a family to take care of. It took many years to process all she learned during that time. The most important things were to have faith, and to remember her ability to be her own leader.

While traveling in the U.S., she met her husband-to-be and followed him to Montana, where she still resides. They had two kids, her most valuable gifts, Tosh and Gabrielle. In 1997, feeling as if her soul was drowning, she divorced her husband. She soon found herself again in a position of leadership; she was now 36 years old. Everything was easier at home; one of the first rules she set up in the house was no more yelling.

Playing music was something she had forgotten and now could enjoy once more. Self-discovery was happening, with questions like; what am I going to do when I grow up? She always had a feeling that she could do something bigger in life than being a wife and serving one person; she wanted to help many.

After taking classes in Aromatherapy, Francoise enrolled in a massage school to combine both modalities. This would allow her to set her own schedule and be with her kids after school. Massage school was a blessing for her, it allowed her to heal her soul and process unresolved issues that were locked up in her body, with no pills, just body work. It made her aware of the load she was carrying.

Her emotional state was getting heavier every time she had to face her ex-husband. She was left drained mentally, emotionally and spiritually for days. She starting paying attention to her emotional state and realized that she was spending most of her time fighting guilt, anger, depression, anxiety and all the many negative thoughts her brain would come up with.

It was with her best friend Anger that she finally put a stop to all that fighting. All she could say was, no more. No more guilt, no more anxiety, no more depression and no more negative. By that time she knew the disguise of anger and welcomed its power. She started to catch her negative thoughts – they were many but she was successful and feeling a lot better. With the support of Star Fire massage school, she focused on getting better. What she experienced, witnessed and learned there inspired her to become an intuitive healer. The understanding was that before the student could help heal others they first needed to heal themselves, and they did; everybody in the class processed their problems and emotional baggage, guided by our teachers and supporting one another through massage and bodywork.

Beside teaching classes of anatomy, physiology, they also taught classes like Reiki and energy work, leading students to develop their intuitive ability. The student would practice and evaluate their intuition during classes. It was mind boggling to see what kind of information they came up with and how accurate they were.

Francoise will always remember one of their first practices. One person was lying on the floor and the rest of the students surrounded him just trying to come up with any kind of info. They would sit there in silence and after few minutes, they would share their finding. When her turn came up, she saw a little baby girl lying on his belly. She didn't know what it meant until the student said "I can't believe it, I was waiting for the end of the day to announce that my wife is pregnant and we are having a baby girl!" Whoa, that was amazing; Francoise was sold, and she put that intuitive tool in her toolbox!

Over the years, Francoise perfected that newfound tool, always helped by instant feedback from her patient, who would validate the information. She realized that she was able to read the energy she felt when putting her hands on their body and what she felt was mostly associated with an emotion like Anger, Anxiety, Depression and Guilt.

She then started to share her methods to help people manage their negative emotions and again with instant feedback she knew she was making a difference in people's lives. Francoise received phone calls from clients thanking her for changing their life and telling her how easy her method was to apply. Many of them had tried therapy; many of them just could not afford it and many of them did not want anything to do with pills.

The biggest complaint for people who had done therapy and read many self-help books was the methods. They would tell me "have you tried to meditate, relax, visualize when you are under the spell of anxiety, anger, depression or guilt; it just does not work. I cannot do it when under attack. But I can catch my teacher, shut it up, breath and relax, then I can investigate the situation."

The most common feedback that Francoise received was how easy this method is and that people could use it anywhere and everywhere all by themselves. Just by remembering the first step: Catch your teacher and shut it up – was all they needed to be successful. By using this method, Francoise was able to let go of all her negative emotions every time they knocked on her door. This left her with a lot more free time to think about the things that mattered to her.

Things like what to do with her life now, and how she could help others find their own peace of mind. Her gift to you is this simple and practical guide to help to free your mind of negative thoughts and re-invest it in something that will bring back a positive return.

Curriculum Vitae

Certified Medical Massage Therapist
Certified 2004
American Medical Massage Therapy Association
Annapolis, Maryland

Certified Massage Therapist, National Certification
Certified since 1998
Board For Therapeutic Massage and Bodywork
McLean, Virginia

Reiki Master
Certified 1998
Jacob Paisain, Independent Reiki Master
Missoula, Montana

Massage Therapist
Certified 1997
Star Fire Massage School
Missoula, Montana

Acupressure Practitioner
Certified 1997
High Touch Network
Friday Harbor, Washington

Certified Aromatherapist
Certified 1996
The Australasian College of Herbal Studies
Lake Oswego, Oregon

According to the National Institute of Mental Health, over 50 million people age 18 or older in this country are affected by mental disorders. Nearly half have more than one disorder. *The Little Toolbox* looks at four emotions commonly associated with mental disorders: anger, anxiety, depression, and guilt. What is the purpose of these emotions?

In *The Little Toolbox* the reader will learn firsthand from the emotion's viewpoint. Francoise impersonates these emotions as great teachers, experts, whose stories have not been told and whose stories will reveal their true nature, their purpose, their wisdom and their disguise. She shares their secrets and defends their potential to teach us.

Anxiety will turn the reader into a private investigator, asking them to find fact or concrete evidence that something is really wrong. It will teach the reader to discern between fact and fiction.

Anger has the best disguise and is my favorite mentor. Anger asks us to feel it and not associate it with negativity. Anger tells us: "Recycle me; I am power, your power."

Depression asks us to pay attention to our forgotten soul. We will work with this teacher on pleasing our senses, our physical being. Our mind cannot resist and will soon follow.

Guilt asks us to look at our intentions and question them. Guilt also offers the reader a chance to investigate their actions and find solid evidence to see whether the guilt is justified or not.

The reader will learn how to consciously set up "pop-up blockers" in their minds to filter and eliminate unwanted thoughts. The reader will gather many tools along the way and create their own toolbox. They will play a game called "Catch your teacher and shut him/her up."